James Clarke

The Pocket Essential

GEORGE LUCAS

www.pocketessentials.com

196720   791-

First published in Great Britain 2002 by Pocket Essentials, 18 Coleswood Road,
Harpenden, Herts, AL5 1EQ   430233
                                  LUC

Distributed in the USA by Trafalgar Square Publishing, PO Box 257, Howe Hill
Road, North Pomfret, Vermont 05053

A CIP catalogue record for this book is available from the British Library.

ISBN 1-903047-94-3

2 4 6 8 10 9 7 5 3 1

Book typeset by Wordsmith Solutions Ltd
Printed and bound by Cox & Wyman

This one is for my grandparents, who have cared from far and near, and for these friends who have encouraged me along the way: John and Sue Pheasant, Chad, John, Mark, Paula, Stephen, Kathy and David Bayly, Rachel McDonald and Al Puente, Russ Sheath, Louise Brosnan, Nick Duffy, Leigh Hughes, Jess McKenzie, Neil Oseman, Chris Mayall, Sarah Laws, Dave Sewell, Eleanor Watling, Justine and Stephen Ryley, David Groves, Sarah Holland, Mike Brady, Nick Ashwell, Susanna Pfeifer, Julian Hall, Julia Goldsmith and, finally, the pal who has shown me the way time and time again, Rick Goldsmith.

CONTENTS

'It is not down on any map. True places never are.'

Herman Melville

'There was things which he stretched,
 but mainly he told the truth.'

Mark Twain, *Huckleberry Finn*

"Films are not films to me. They are life…you learn."

Martin Scorsese

1: Maverick
George Lucas' Fast Life And Times

"You know the brittle bough breaks. The willow bends with the wind and stays on the tree. You try to fight it...and you lose. You're not going to remain eighteen forever."

George Lucas,
interview with Larry Sturhahn,
The Filming Of American Graffiti, 1973

A wide-eyed kid gazes longingly at the suns setting. A wide-eyed kid gazes longingly at his mother as he leaves her. A wide-eyed archaeologist grins with the satisfaction of discovery and understanding. An escaped future man stands against the sunrise. A wide-eyed teenager realises that everything changes. More than all the visual bells and whistles that ice every George Lucas movie, what drives his most brilliant efforts are very simple and emotionally direct stories about growing up. It just happens to be that the growing-up happens whilst hurtling through the stars or fleeing a robotic police force or criss-crossing the globe. There is consistency in these films, something singular. A George Lucas movie is not an easy thing to miss, and not just because of the attendant hype. Lucas' films are distinctively pieced together, in their character types and visual dynamism.

In September 2001, on the official Lucasfilm/*Star Wars* website George Lucas quietly announced the title of his new film. It would be called *Star Wars: Episode II: Attack Of The Clones*. Within minutes a wave of debate and response filled cyberspace. After almost thirty years Lucas continues to connect with masses of movie-goers and film fans.

In 2002, Lucas released his fifth movie in 31 years as a writer/director. Alongside Terrence Malick, director of *Badlands*, *Days Of Heaven* and *The Thin Red Line*, Lucas is the most deliberate and, in a way, aesthetically pure of the so-called Movie Brat directors who blasted into cinemas back in the early 1970s. Lucas' cadre included Martin Scorsese, Steven Spielberg, Brian De Palma, John Milius and Francis Ford Coppola. Unlike his contemporaries, Lucas has not adapted a novel into a feature film and only directs screenplays that he has written. Also, his principal Lucasfilm features come from Lucas' work as a writer and ideas generator.

Lucas has been decried for using clunky dialogue and simplistically rehashing pulpy formulae with no real ambition. In fairness, Lucas has always admitted that screenwriting is not his greatest strength - he shapes the sequences and rhythms of his stories at the editing stage.

Lucas is a story archaeologist who gathers and reworks storytelling forms and narrative devices from other films, TV serials, mythological tales, comic books and old rock and roll songs. He dusts them down and represents them to contemporary audiences like a modern version of the Brothers Grimm. Lucas has said his connection with a mass sensibility has been more significant than the skill, or otherwise, of his film-making craft.

Like Steven Spielberg, Lucas has been branded one of the reasons Hollywood cinema became so juvenile during the early 1980s. For many this is a situation from which mainstream film-making will never recover. In her review of *Raiders Of The Lost Ark*, film critic Pauline Kael (who raved about *Star Wars: Episode V: The Empire Strikes Back*) talked of Lucas being 'hooked on the crap of his childhood' rather than making films with real people in them.

Lucas has a style (fast pacing, simple storylines, young protagonists and upbeat conclusions) that is assuredly his. Time and again audiences want to immerse themselves in the kind of stories Lucas tells. As in any form, there are always less able imitators who can give a bad name to the best exponents. Maybe that attitude reflects a prejudice that critics have against popular culture rather than against Lucas. Lucas grew up in an era when America adored its pop culture in mass production, television, music and film. Lucas celebrates his past by updating it for the current popular culture audience.

In a typically American way, Lucas has never dubbed himself an artist. Instead, he describes himself as a craftsman who makes the film he is interested in and from thereon it is others' choice to attach certain kinds of meaning to it. In his films, Lucas creates self-contained and believable worlds which are enriched by the fact that, in many cases, he has followed the characters as they grow up. The clearest example of this is the mammoth *Star Wars* saga, in which we follow the Skywalker family across time and a galaxy. Lucas even followed some of the characters from *American Graffiti* in the film *More American Graffiti*. With Indiana Jones, Lucas showed us the archaeologist's formative years in an expansive and intelligent TV series in the early 1990s. Tellingly, Lucas documents his fictions as though they live and breathe in our real world. In his early days, he made documentaries and the spirit of that form has never left him.

Several of Lucas' films (some as writer/director, some as creator/ producer) have been immensely successful. Yet, he has had fewer hits than misses. The hits have been so vast that a range of quirky and interesting films have got lost in the shuffle.

For children growing up in the 1970s, Lucas' film *Star Wars* (later retitled *Star Wars: Episode IV: A New Hope*) introduced them to cinema and fantasy. One suspects that recent releases like *Harry Potter And The Philosopher's Stone* or *The Lord Of The Rings: The Fellowship Of The Ring* will do the same for a whole new generation. One hopes so. Many of the kids from the 1970s went on to pursue careers in creative industries and film-making, and were the first in line 22 years later when *Star Wars: Episode I: The Phantom Menace* was released, hoping in a somewhat misguided way that the film would mean everything to them that the original *Star Wars* had. Sadly, how could it? Nostalgia can be a blessing and a curse.

Lucas' stories have not only entertained and inspired many young minds but have shaped the course of their careers. Lucas is a figurehead for many because of the struggles he went through to build his career. He started as a guerrilla film-maker alongside Francis Ford Coppola when they filmed *The Rain People* in Nebraska in 1968. An independent film-maker from the beginning (and he still is, it is just that the huge commercial success masks this position a little), Lucas was never based in Hollywood. He had contacts and colleagues there but he quit town as soon as he finished film school and established himself in the San Francisco area alongside Francis Ford Coppola. With their film-making friends and colleagues they established American Zoetrope with Lucas as Vice Chairman, watching and learning from Coppola.

Lucas had suggested calling the company TransAmerican Sprocket Works but that was regarded as too cute.

From all accounts, Lucas struggled to get his first feature *THX 1138* made. It was the same story with *American Graffiti* and *Star Wars*. Now in the twenty-first century Lucas is leading the way to stop using film and to make movies with digital cameras. To some this seems like heresy, but it marks the same shift as the introduction of sound, then colour and finally the manufacture of smaller, portable cameras. Economics and industry always impact on the kinds of art that we create. For Lucas, digital and high definition video is the next logical step, being cheaper than film and easier to manage, manipulate and archive. Throughout his career Lucas has used and improved technology. His second film as writer/director, *American Graffiti*, was the first to use videotape in the audition process. In the 1980s Lucasfilm developed EditDroid, a non-linear edit system that ran on a computer, basing the editing process around cutting and pasting images just as we cut and paste text daily on our computers. Today it is the post-production norm for most production companies. Slowly but surely other directors are beginning to embrace the prospects of digital cinema such as Mike Figgis with *Timecode,* Lars Von Trier, Robert Rodriguez and Steven Soderbergh. Just as Lucas and many of his colleagues were good adverts for going to film school, their use of digital technology encourages people to make films at home. To an extent there are now no excuses not to make a film or, more correctly, a digital movie. Why bother with film school anymore when you can have a mini studio environment at home? This revolutionary situation has made film-making more democratic and ties into Lucas' long-held rallying cry for independence. Interestingly, in an interview in 1983 with Aljean Hermetz, Lucas talked very positively about digital technology allowing for more regional film-making. You now no longer have to be in Hollywood or even a big city to devise, shoot and complete a film.

As David Thomson notes in his terrific *Biographical Dictionary Of Film*, Lucas is a potent example of the producer in American mainstream cinema. James Schamus, writer and producer of several Ang Lee films, is a similar example. Lucas has conceived and executive-produced many films outside of his most famous efforts. Away from the all-powerful Skywalker saga Lucas has been involved in other films that have been different and quixotic.

Since the success of *A New Hope*, Lucas' commitment has frequently focused on creating films for young minds. In several more recent interviews, Lucas has referred to the concept of emotional intelligence as developed and described by psychologist Daniel Goleman in his book, *Emotional Intelligence*. Developing this facility in children has clearly been a powerful motive behind Lucas' work on the first three episodes of the *Star Wars* story. Of course, Lucas' commitment to stories that encourage and foster positivity has been there since *American Graffiti*. Audiences wrote to Lucas saying they felt better at the end of the movie. Lucas was encouraged by this as a sign of films' potential for positive impact. With the *Star Wars* 'prequels' Lucas follows the early years of the man who became Darth Vader. Whilst certainly drawing on mythological devices (as he did first time around), Lucas is also exploring how young people deal with the highs and lows of the heart and mind. It is fair to say that with his *Star Wars* films there is an apparent mission to make them work as 'educational' tools for children. Lucas' best movies compel young people to think beyond the everyday. Screenwriter and director Frank Darabont, who worked with Lucas on *The Young Indiana Jones Chronicles* and who was approached to write *The Phantom Menace*, famously described Lucas as "Yoda in sneakers."

For some though, Lucas' benign and reserved image disguises what some see as a cynical operation, driven by the commercial potential in merchandising his films. As Lucas himself acknowledges, the merchandising is a way to maintain the work of his company. From *A New Hope* onwards, Lucas' high-profile films have had some serious tie-in potential, extending even to theme park attraction at the Disneyland and Disneyworld sites - proof that Lucas' *Star Wars* and *Indiana Jones* worlds are very much bona fide features of the American pop culture landscape. They have a place on the Mount Rushmore of American pop phenomena alongside Elvis, Mark Twain and Disney.

When *The Phantom Menace* was released, the hype focused on the hype itself and the film got lost in the scramble. *Attack Of The Clones* has been received more fairly as a film in and of itself.

Lucas has not just built worlds on screen. He has frequently described himself as a frustrated architect. Way back in 1974 he said: "I'm very much akin to a toymaker. If I wasn't a film-maker, I'd probably be a toymaker. I like to make things move and I like to make them myself."(Stephen Farber, 'George Lucas: The Stinky Kid Hits The Big Time,' *Film Quarterly*, spring 1974, pp. 2-9) Lucas is as famous for building worlds in reality as in fiction.

In 1980 construction began in Northern California on Lucas' administrative, design, writing and post-production facility Skywalker Ranch. Lucas has made an environment that encourages people to focus their creative energy. Some journalists' accounts of the ranch indicate it is too untouched by the outside world, which is perhaps a sad reflection on today's tendency towards endless distraction.

Before Skywalker Ranch, and even before *Star Wars* hit screens in 1977, there was the foundation of what remains the byword for visual effects: Industrial Light and Magic. Using some of the profits from *American Graffiti*, Lucas established ILM to create material for *A New Hope*. What began in a warehouse facility in 1976 in Van Nuys, Southern California, has grown into a world centre of movie-making effects. Initially ILM was a one-off venture where part of the work was not just to create effects but to create the equipment to realise the images. In 1979 ILM moved north to San Rafael, Northern California. Many of the star craftspeople at ILM continue either at the company (notably Dennis Muren, Steve Gawley and Lorne Peterson) or have made other marks on the film-making industry (*Star Wars* designer Joe Johnston is the director of fine fantasy films, *Honey I Shrunk The Kids*, *The Rocketeer*, *Jumanji*, *October Sky* and *Jurassic Park 3*). Today, ILM contributes effects for movies and commercials, and has demonstrated that visual effects can help make movies cheaper, not more expensive. The photorealism and seamlessness of so much computer-generated effects work mean that we can be immersed in the attack on Pearl Harbour or that we can watch a man who never really met JFK go and meet JFK. Believability and the boundaries of the cinema of wonder are frequently being redefined by ILM's work.

Since the early 1980s Lucas has also been involved in computer gaming and the LucasArts Entertainment Company is a major force in the industry. Less high profile, but maybe the most valuable of all Lucas' projects, is the work of The George Lucas Educational Foundation which promotes the use of digital media in the formal American school system. It uses technology to develop communication, teaching and community interaction.

Lucas' films and other projects celebrate community and diversity and are quintessentially American in their energy and enthusiasm. He is the L Frank Baum of American popular cinema.

2: Growing Up

Robots, fairy tales, archaeology, adventure. All of these are a long way from 14 May 1944 when George Walton Lucas Jr. was born in the little town of Modesto in the San Joaquin Valley, California. As with so many famous names, Lucas' formative years have assumed a mythology of their own.

Growing up with three sisters, Lucas appears to have led a pretty stable and secure life. His father ran the local stationery and supply store (LM Morris), hoping perhaps that one day his only son would take over the business. Lucas famously told his father, dubious about his son's later decision to go to film school, that he would be a millionaire by the time he was 30. As a kid Lucas became hooked on more exciting things than life in Modesto. First there was the arrival of TV and viewing countless serials such as *Flash Gordon*, *Buck Rogers* and *Don Winslow*. Radio was also a constant and there were comic books too. And then there was rock and roll. Feature films were less of a force for Lucas as a child. When *A New Hope* was first released Lucas showed the Chuck Jones' Daffy Duck classic *Duck Dodgers In The 24½th Century* before it. Steven Spielberg joked in a 2001 *Omnibus* (BBC TV) documentary about Chuck Jones that Marvin the Martian was Lucas' inspiration for the design of Darth Vader. The torrent of TV adventure Lucas watched as a kid continues to find its way into his films. In *The Phantom Menace* the video screen on which Queen Amidala appears at the very beginning is a direct reference to the screens seen in the old *Flash Gordon* shows.

As Lucas edged towards his teens the thrill and speed of cars consumed almost every waking hour and he had ambitions to work in the car industry. Lucas spent much of his free time cruising Modesto in his supped-up Fiat. He did not find school engaging and his artistic temperament began to shine through as he developed an interest and facility with photography and illustration. On 18 June 1962, Lucas' life took a turn for the worse and then a turn for the better. Driving along the highway his car flipped and got acquainted with a tree. Lucas' seatbelt broke and he was flung from the car to safety. After being hospitalised Lucas recognised how lucky he had been and he made a vow to use his time more wisely. Everything, notably time, suddenly seemed a lot more precious than it had before. Lucas enrolled at college and began studying with a vengeance, his subjects including anthropology, astronomy and literature. In 1992 Steven Spielberg presented Lucas with the Irving J Thalberg Award at the Oscars for excellence in film production. The accolade was fitting beyond its industry context. Thalberg, who ran MGM studios in the 1920s and 1930s as a very young man, also felt he was living on borrowed time because of his poor heart condition. Tellingly, Lucas' acceptance of the Thalberg award gave him the chance to thank his teachers, making concrete his career-long commitment to using the student/teacher dynamic as a focal point in his stories.

At the age of 20, with the encouragement of a sportscar fan, friend and cinematographer Haskell Wexler, Lucas applied to the University of Southern California in Los Angeles and got accepted onto its three-year film programme. Lucas had never been an all-knowing film fan in the way Spielberg and Scorsese had been. Instead, Lucas' interest stemmed from still photography, which to some degree informs the often uncluttered and static visual design of his motion picture frames. Lucas' films achieve their sense of motion through edited images rather than by moving the camera.

As Lucas has acknowledged, he found his niche at USC and dedicated all his energies to film-making. The same zeal he had shown for motor cars came through in his work and he swiftly became the star student with films such as *Anyone Lived In A Pretty How Town*, *Look At Life* (a rapidly cut montage of photos from *Life* magazine, driven by a kinetic rhythmic beat) and *Freiheit* (*Freedom*), a title indicating things to come in his feature work. Lucas' focus on animation at film school returned on *The Phantom Menace* where Lucas made a movie that focused, in almost every frame, on fusing live action and animation. In many ways this aesthetic remains the heart of special effects.

At USC, Lucas enjoyed using the camera and editing, but he was less interested in narrative film-making in the classic Hollywood tradition. In 1997, Lucas referred to his "theatrical immersion" on his work on *Star Wars*.

Whilst studying, Lucas befriended John Milius and Walter Murch, amongst others. Lucas even met a guy studying English at Long Beach

State who had not been able to get accepted at film school. His name was Steven Spielberg. Lucas remained at USC for a Masters and supplemented his work by teaching there. Whilst training Navy soldiers in film-making he saw an opportunity to make use of what was essentially a ready-made crew and embarked on his 20-minute short film, *THX 1138 4EB: Electronic Labyrinth*. The film won many awards and led to Lucas getting a scholarship with Warner Brothers. The film was the germ for his debut feature *THX 1138* (1971).

At Warner Brothers, Lucas observed the death of the studio system whilst watching a range of films, including the desert adventure *McKenna's Gold*, being shot. Whilst on the set of *Finian's Rainbow*, a musical starring Petula Clark, Tommy Steele and Fred Astaire, he swiftly struck up a friendship with the young director, Francis Ford Coppola. Soon afterwards, Coppola began a more personal film, *The Rain People*, starring a very young James Caan. Coppola, impressed by Lucas, brought him on board as an assistant. Lucas did whatever was needed on the production as it rolled across the Midwest. Before each day's shoot, between about 4 a.m. and 6 a.m., Lucas would work on the script for what he hoped would be his first feature, *THX 1138*. He also found time to make a documentary about Coppola called *Filmmaker*.

After *The Rain People* shoot, which was a model for the way to make future movies (small crew, mobile equipment), Coppola established a film-making operation in Northern California that was geographically and 'spiritually' removed from Hollywood. Calling the company American Zoetrope the original dream was to be based in a rural location, inspired by the example of their film-maker friend John Korty. An office building on Folsom Street in San Francisco became the eventual base and Lucas was installed as Vice President. The cadre of young film-makers included Carol Ballard and Robert Dalva, who went on to successful Hollywood careers. Ballard directed two terrific films for kids, *The Black Stallion* and *Fly Away Home*. Dalva emerged as an editor, most recently on *Jurassic Park 3*. Walter Murch co-wrote and sound-designed *THX 1138*, worked as sound designer on *The Godfather* films, *The Conversation*, *Apocalypse Now* and more recently edited *The Unbearable Lightness Of Being* and *The English Patient*.

Half a dozen scripts were developed by Zoetrope and submitted to Warner Brothers in a fancy black box. *THX 1138* was one of the scripts and, with Coppola on board as producer, it received a green light, going into production in late 1969. The movie was finally released in 1971 and received its share of critical praise. It was not a hit, although it did recoup its budget. Today *THX 1138* has something of a cult following. The film's commercial failure made Lucas feel as though he was back where he started as he watched the careers of his colleagues and friends take off. Coppola took a job for hire on a film called *The Godfather*, partly to pay back debts he and Zoetrope had incurred from the unproduced scripts that Warners had bought and then rejected after *THX 1138*'s release.

Despite financial strains, Lucas was adamant that he would only make the films he wanted to. His wife at the time, Marcia Lucas, began to get high-profile editing jobs, working with Scorsese on *Alice Doesn't Live Here Anymore* and *Taxi Driver*. Lucas took camera operating jobs, such as shooting some of the DA Pennebaker film *Gimme Shelter*, the documentary of The Rolling Stones concert at Altamont. Lucas also worked on some sequences of *The Godfather*, notably the montage of newspaper titles. At one point Lucas worked in the studio of ace title animator Saul Bass.

Recognising Lucas' skills as a film-maker, Coppola encouraged him to write something warmer and more personal. Lucas took this as a challenge, given his initial impulse towards non narrative work. Lucas developed an outline for *American Graffiti* and refined it with longstanding pals and colleagues from his USC days, Willard Huyck and Gloria Katz. He faced some stiff opposition to the project, because the studios were uneasy with the multi-character, 'revolving' plot - a device we now see daily on TV dramas. Lucas dubbed the movie a 'musical,' not because the characters stopped and sang but because it pounded with a stream of rock and roll songs from the late 1950s and early 1960s. The film was eventually given the go-ahead by Universal Pictures. It was a smash hit and Lucas began to consider his next project, a Vietnam-set story inspired by the Joseph Conrad novel *Heart Of Darkness*. Lucas' intention was to shoot it vérité style on 16mm film in the Philippines from John Milius' screenplay. The plan did not pan out so

Francis Ford Coppola took over the project that became *Apocalypse Now*. Walter Murch has accurately stated that in some ways Lucas went on to transfer some of the issues of *Apocalypse Now* to outer space in the project he began developing as he basked in the warmth of *American Graffiti*'s success.

Lucas' previous two films had been shot on location, but he wanted to film his space adventure on lavish studio sets. Finally overcoming the now-familiar resistance of studios, Lucas went into production in London in March 1976, about the same time as Coppola began *Apocalypse Now* in The Philippines. Lucas' film, *Star Wars*, was released in May 1977. Coppola endured numerous traumas in the production of *Apocalypse Now*, finally releasing it in 1979. To Lucas' surprise *Star Wars* was hugely popular, becoming the most commercially successful film ever made. It swiftly became a phenomenon, developing a life way beyond its roots as a film and becoming the movie for which Lucas will forever be remembered. In a 1999 web documentary on the official *Star Wars* website, John Williams referred to the *Star Wars* saga as "a life's work journey" for Lucas.

With *Star Wars* ensuring Lucas' freedom, he began developing and diversifying his work and interests, which some have viewed with a hint of regret. In a BBC documentary screened in 1997, *Flying Solo*, Coppola said that after *Star Wars*, American cinema lost one of its brightest talents as a director when Lucas concentrated on building a media company and developing projects as a producer. In the afterglow of *Star Wars*, Lucas began talking intensely about wanting to shoot far less theatrically inclined films, to return to his roots of pure, non-narrative, more abstract film. If he ever does so it would be intriguing. Perhaps Lucas' special effects sequences, with their immense graphic impact, are partly a way to satisfy this creative ambition. No dialogue, just movement, colour and sound.

After *Star Wars*, Lucas decided to tell the story of the *American Graffiti* characters in the late 1960s in *More American Graffiti*. Its original proposed title had been *Purple Haze*. Of the first film's stars only Richard Dreyfuss did not put in an appearance. Again the story was set around multiple storylines following each character but the scenarios were inherently less zestful than those of the first film. Lucas was the film's executive producer and devised the story. He also directed second unit Vietnam footage in California, in a sense maybe getting to make his own mini *Apocalypse Now*. *More American Graffiti* was released in 1979 but did not prove too popular.

With audiences eager for more space adventure, and Lucas equally keen to continue telling his story, he released *The Empire Strikes Back* in 1980. This time Lucas conceived the story, oversaw the production as executive producer and hired Irvin Kershner to direct. Again, Lucas had another mammoth hit on his hands and he followed it up in 1981 with *Raiders Of The Lost Ark* (directed by Steven Spielberg, retitled *Indiana Jones And The Raiders Of The Lost Ark* in 2000) which was the biggest draw of the year. Lucas had conceived the character of Indiana Jones (or Smith as he was originally monikered) in the early 1970s whilst developing *Star Wars*. A thrilling action adventure movie, the film revived the genre but was also seen as yet another nail in the coffin of mature American cinema. Looking back, the film was an action movie watershed and the genre has been consistently revised ever since.

Lucas also oversaw the development of a subdivision of Lucasfilm called Pixar, dedicated to computer-generated images under the supervision of Ed Catmull, a computer animation specialist at a time when it was a new frontier. In the mid-1980s Pixar was sold to Apple head-honcho, Steve Jobs and a long time later Pixar gave the world *Toy Story*, *A Bug's Life*, *Tin Toy*, *Luxo Jr.* and *Monsters Inc*.

In 1983, Lucas released *Star Wars: Episode VI: Return Of The Jedi*, the final instalment of the *Star Wars* series. The film clarified Lucas' interest in anthropology - he likes to think of the films as documentaries of a fictional culture. Lucas hit the jackpot again with *Return Of The Jedi* and he was apparently getting a little embarrassed by the popularity of his work.

Lucas not only used the profits from the movies and the merchandising to fund his films but also to fund the development of more streamlined film-making technology. By 1982, ILM had begun to investigate the potential of computer graphics in *Star Trek II: The Wrath Of Khan*. By 2002, computer graphics have become an everyday aspect of movies, though they are often used to be invisible rather than to show the birth of a planet or the twisting of Meryl Streep's head in Robert

Zemeckis' *Death Becomes Her*. Technology has allowed for the creation of the digital backlot, whereby an environment is created in a computer rather than being physically built at full scale. Even crowd scenes may only involve the smallest number of people in front of the film camera. The computer will then replicate them in their hundreds, thousands and millions if needed.

Lucas, along with other digital cinema pioneers and advocators, has kept the form fluid and adaptable. In the process he has perhaps helped make it a more democratic medium, removing it from the stranglehold of the corporations. Digital video is swiftly resulting in the creation of a more diverse range of content, rather like the impact cheap music technology had when it allowed people to build music studios at home.

Throughout his career, Lucas has remained true to the issues and formats that mean the most to him. It is evident that he is engaged by the process of creating the film rather than what the film might say. He has not bowed to Hollywood expectation and made obviously 'meaningful' films. Every movie and every story has meaning. In Lucas' movies, the characters are absolutely defined by their actions, by their appearance. These are visual films, amongst the least pretentious ever made. There is a kind of humility to them.

So what makes a movie a George Lucas movie? Given that much of his work has an element of fantasy to it Lucas has truly found a way to make the fantasy seem completely real - the unfamiliar is made familiar. In a film such as Spielberg's *Close Encounters Of The Third Kind* (1977) the familiar is made unfamiliar, perhaps highlighting one of the essential differences between these two very different film-makers - early in their careers their names were interchanged with alarming ignorance by the mainstream press. Aside from an often very vivid sense of vérité to films directed by Lucas, his screenplays, screen stories and films tend to focus on the following ideas: community, self-belief and the realisation of potential, respect for an established system and tradition, and the good and bad voice of the past. An unquestioning adherence to established paths and powers always proves dangerous in his films. The *Star Wars* universe is pluralist - all life forms are worthy of respect. His films tend to project an ethos of peace and harmony, celebrating the power of sacrifice, guardianship and compassion. Whilst these issues are not dealt with in any overly complex way they are present and expansive enough to give the movies an emotional believability and relevance. To paraphrase Lucas' refrain: a special effect without a story is a pretty boring thing. It is not inaccurate to suggest that the reason the *Star Wars* films have connected so vividly with viewers is probably mostly due to the concept of The Force, frequently regarded as a rough guide of sorts to the essential ideas of religions. Of all the faiths and teachings it suggests and references, the spirit of Zen is perhaps the strongest. It was certainly what director Irvin Kershner used as his model for *The Empire Strikes Back*. For those whose interest in the possibilities of Zen were sparked by Lucas' *Star Wars* stories then seek out the books *Zen Flesh, Zen Bones* and *Zen In The Art Of Archery*. Yoda surely keeps these on his bookshelf.

There have been countless films with visual effects as good as those in the *Star Wars* films but they have not had anything like the staying power of the Skywalker saga. This is because of the emotional reference points in the story (doubt, anger, patience, logic, family ties (for better and for worse), freedom, self-potential, friendship, commitment) are the very ideas and feelings we experience and grapple with in our daily lives.

Some of Lucas' stories explore the pursuit of ambition, the realisation of it and the price paid for it. Strong women populate his films as does speed whether it is the speed of narrative, the speed of vehicles or the speed of dialogue. Things don't stand still too long in a Lucas film. Part of the main characters' strength is the way they deal with an onslaught of chaos and energy. Life is motion. Perhaps Han Solo's flight of the Millennium Falcon through the asteroid belt in *The Empire Strikes Back* is the quintessential Lucas sequence. Interestingly, in a 1989 interview critics Ebert and Siskel asked Lucas for an image from his films that defined him. He did not answer with one. Instead, Lucas referenced the editing pattern of the TIE fighter attack on the Millennium Falcon in *Star Wars*. Spielberg and Scorsese were also interviewed for the same book and readily answered with specific images from their films. Lucas' roots as an editor rather than as a writer or director of performers are worth remembering when you watch his films, particularly those he has directed. Where Spielberg or Scorsese might invest the frame with energy through a moving camera, Lucas tends to keep his camera locked off and removed from the action. For Lucas the energy is created through editing patterns; that is where Lucas' creative freedom lies. A certain silent movie aesthetic also threads through his work as director. As Lucas acknowledged upon the release of *The Phantom Menace*, John Williams' orchestral score operates in the way a musical accompaniment does to a silent film. This is one reason for the film's huge appeal. Music exists and works beyond spoken language and the cultural barriers that creates. The use of music amplifies Lucas' cinematic approach. Many people who recall seeing *A New Hope* when it was first released had a very clear sense of what was happening but were not focused on the dialogue, supporting Lucas' claim to a silent film approach where the pictures speak for themselves. Hitchcock worked to the same fundamental principle. The other appeal Lucas' work surely has to young minds is the framing of all life experience as an energetic adventure of trials and successes, gains and losses. Lucas has frequently maintained an interest in the power of mythology and he has employed certain mythological devices to structure his stories. He has openly acknowledged a particular debt to the late Joseph Campbell and his book *The Hero With A Thousand Faces*. In the wake of *Star Wars'* success, Campbell became a celebrity and his work was endlessly referenced.

After completing the second *Star Wars* trilogy (Lucas said he had only outlined two trilogies), Lucas became involved in a wider range of projects usually as an executive producer. As Lucasfilm continued to produce films, LucasArts Entertainment Company became a major presence in computer gaming and ILM continued to define quality in special effects.

Lucas made his much-heralded return to directing in June 1997 after spending almost three years researching, developing and writing the screenplay for *The Phantom Menace*. There was no way the expectation could be met. Now that the dust of hype has settled, the film stands as a strong entry in the *Star Wars* series. Clearly many fans (especially those familiar with the spin-off books and comics) expected the kind of darkness present in those stories.

As far back as 1989 Lucas announced he would begin work on the *Star Wars* prequels, at one point suggesting they would be released around 1997 and might even be filmed back-to-back. Most importantly, Lucas stated they would have more intrigue and complication to them, more darkness, than the second trilogy. What many expected was perhaps the darkness of the duel between Luke and Vader at the end of *The Empire Strikes Back* stretched over two hours. Instead, *The Phantom Menace* was a bright, energetic and colourful blast between forests, deserts and cities with a somewhat nihilistic undercurrent. The film was released to largely negative reviews but now, with the smoke of expectation cleared, audiences can take a fresh look at the film.

Lucas' movies as writer/director are essentially American in their issues, form and feeling, and in their celebration of youth and energy. They possess what Walt Whitman would call snap and fling. Having derived from past popular culture, Lucas' films are now potent examples of current popular culture. Having generated relics in the form of merchandising, toys, clocks, books ad infinitum, the series is now recognised by elite thinkers around the world. Lucas' work has become enshrined in the culture through museum exhibits. In October 1997 The Smithsonian Institution in Washington hosted *Star Wars: The Magic Of Myth* exhibition which placed *Star Wars* in the grand tradition of world mythology, and *The Art Of Star Wars* exhibit toured America and the UK in 1999/2000.

Whether it's a yellow Deuce Coupe roaring down Paradise Road or a yellow starfighter rocketing across a blue sky, the Lucas film story is the same: get out into the world, make your mark, be your own person. As Lucas himself has said: "If you set your goals too high, then they are impossible to reach. You just get frustrated. So you set them as high as is realistic - not impossible but very difficult. As corny as it sounds, the power of positive thinking goes a long way."

3: Being A Kid Is Great - Films As Writer/Director

"I'm not stopping to explain anything ever."

George Lucas, 1979

THX 1138 (1971)

Cast: Robert Duvall (THX), Maggie McOmie (LUH), Donald Pleasence (SEN), Don Pedro Colley (Hologram).

Crew: Director: George Lucas; Screenplay: George Lucas & Walter Murch from a screen story by George Lucas; Producer: Lawrence Sturhahn; Executive Producer: Francis Ford Coppola; Sound Design: Walter Murch; Cinematography: Al Kihn & Dave Myers; Additional Photography: Haskell Wexler; Music: Lalo Schifrin; Editor: George Lucas. American Zoetrope/Warner Brothers. 95 mins.

Story: In an unspecified future - antiseptic and subterranean - the populace are controlled and suppressed by sedation, allowing them to go about their existence without pain, risk or the complications of emotion. Under constant surveillance and soothed by the unknown voice of an all-seeing, all-knowing 'phantom,' the men and women go about their duties operating technology. A faceless police force, armed with stun sticks, patrol the world, reinforcing the order. A couple, THX and LUH, live in their antiseptic apartment, watching holographic 'TV' images - their lives endlessly soundtracked by an omnipresent, omniscient superpower. THX and LUH struggle to find a way to express their emotions and THX becomes increasingly uneasy. LUH and THX reduce their pill intake and make love. Subsequently, THX is put on trial and 'imprisoned' in The White Limbo - an all-white world with apparently no boundary. THX is attacked by the police and also subjected to a range of violations to his body by probes, needles and monitors. THX spasms and sits in a daze, as though the victim of some kind of future world electro-shock therapy. Surrounded by other prisoners, endlessly talking about change and rebellion, THX can stand it no more and realises he must liberate himself from this world. With the help of a lumbering hologram, THX makes the break for freedom, against the concerns of SEN, an older, devious and neurotic character. THX makes a rapid escape which SEN wants no part of. On foot and by futuristic police car, THX finally emerges from the underworld into a beautiful sunset.

Themes: The classic Lucas theme of rebellion is paramount in *THX 1138*. THX predates and connects to Curt Henderson in *American Graffiti*, Luke Skywalker in *A New Hope* and Anakin Skywalker in *The Phantom Menace*. THX is a young man who undertakes a journey that sees him liberated and courageous enough to challenge the dominant order. Despite the film's surface austerity and presentation of a bleak future, THX's story is actually a hopeful one, although it has not been realised in a traditionally triumphalist Hollywood style. The film announces many motifs and situations that echo throughout Lucas' directorial career. *THX 1138* contains the seeds of the *Star Wars* saga. The huge stun sticks that the faceless police use make a return appearance when Jar-Jar Binks returns to his home world of Otoh Gunga in *The Phantom Menace*. The police of *THX 1138* also, very obviously, predate the stormtroopers and the Battle Droids. Don Pedro Colley's lumbering partner in escape evokes Chewbacca and Jar-Jar Binks. As SEN makes his way alone he almost uncovers the true identity of the voice which encompasses the world - nothing more than a tape recorder and a photographic blow-up in what looks very much like a TV studio. A hooded, monk-like character expels SEN from the location. Lucas repeats this motif in *American Graffiti* and *The Empire Strikes Back* with Curt's realisation of the true identity of Wolfman Jack and Luke's sudden realisation as to who Yoda is. In all of Lucas' stories, sources of power and influence are often not what they may appear just as The Wizard of Oz is not quite what he seems to be. The subterranean, cloaked troll-like figures suggest the Jawas of Tatooine and the hooded, slowly-walking line of 'monks' predate the appearance of the Jedi Knights. *THX 1138* makes clear Lucas' affinity for narratives built around a trek, a very tangible physical journey which can serve as a way to illustrate the growth of a character as they respond to the various dilemmas and challenges confronting them along the way.

25

Whilst not a comedy, *THX 1138* carries little comic moments. In all his films, Lucas offsets the serious drama with humour. Take, for example, the funny and slightly postmodern moment where THX, SEN and the hologram stand in silhouette at the edge of The White Limbo, very much as though they are on the edge of the film set, rather like Daffy Duck running off the edge of the film. Or the scene when the lift does not work, as an announcement makes clear, and yet people still get into it. There is darker humour at work in the image of the lizard gnawing on the cables connected to the tape playing the 'voice.' The shot has menace, a sense of nature ultimately reigning supreme over the manufactured and controlled. This is Lucas' key theme in *THX 1138* and his other work as a writer/director. When one of the policemen is destroyed in The White Limbo, the screen registers the number of police reduced by one. Consider the almost throwaway scene of the policeman talking to the children with his eerie voice - there is nothing comfortable, warm or protective about him at all.

THX 1138 connects with everyone's occasional sense of being adrift and out of touch. When THX's concern about his relationship (or non-relationship) with LUH reaches a pitch he goes into a booth (rather like a confession box) where an image of Jesus appears in the background accompanied by a monotone, banal voice and series of responses. Tragically, THX believes he is actually being listened to. "How can I be so wrong?" he asks. "My mate has been acting very strange." THX is emoting, being human and the only response he gets from the voice is a monotone, "I understand." Rather than soothe, the voice unsettles. As THX's session ends he looks out of the booth with dismay and the voice states: "Work hard, increase production, prevent accidents and be happy." Lucas' film seems even more true in 2002 than it did in 1971.

Knowledge is power. Lucas' love of ideas and presenting them for the mass audience is apparent in *THX 1138*. The character of SEN says, "One idea could set us free." That could almost be a slogan for all of Lucas' films as a writer and director. SEN babbles like C-3PO. It is THX, the man of deeds not words, who makes the difference. Everything that is not said is where the meaning lies so you read between the lines. Actions do speak louder than words. Tellingly, SEN comments, "Nothing stopped us." When THX, SEN and the hologram finally reach the end of The White Limbo they recognise that only fear was holding them back from breaking free. This is a recurrent Lucas theme. Even a whipcrack-fast movie like *Raiders Of The Lost Ark* allows us to recognise Indiana Jones' determination and integrity on his quest.

Lucas' screen heroes are always mavericks who go their own way and challenge an established order which has been based on fear and no questioning of authority. Lucas' dialogue is not laden with thoughts on this issue. Instead we see the meaning unfold very much through the actions of the characters, through their reactions to situations. The spartan dialogue, when it comes, is terse and almost symbolic rather than naturalistic in its form and function. Lucas has always been criticised for his dialogue, which he himself describes as being functional and subservient to the visual. Intentionally or not, this austere style creates a very specific feeling, reinforcing the film's otherworldly aspect. "I need something stronger," THX says with monotone understatement as he grows increasingly weak, both physically and mentally. In *THX 1138* there is no sense of a guiding supernatural force in the way there is in Lucas' other movies as a director and occasionally as a writer and producer. You could say that THX's sense of integrity and independence is spirit enough.

THX 1138 has always been regarded as a cold film, which is not accurate. The world in which the story is set is indeed cold and chilling, which is the whole point of the tale. However, THX and LUH are very human in their displays of frustration and anger, warmth and tenderness towards one another. A sense of the human in drama does not solely refer to expressions of happy, triumphal, upbeat emotion. *THX 1138* is a very human film, acknowledging the sense of isolation and loneliness felt by everybody, and it is because of this that it is as warm as the Lucas films that followed, just in a different way. *THX 1138* acknowledges, in less effervescent ways than *American Graffiti* and *Star Wars* do, the strength to be found in friendships and intimate relationships. Just look at THX's friendship with the hologram (who predates Chewbacca and Jar-Jar in his innocence). "I'm not real," the hologram says. "I was stuck in the same circuit too long. I always wanted to be part of the real world. So I left." In the virtual cyberworld of 2002, this line is amazingly appropriate. The hologram joins the trek. How brilliant that

Lucas just has him say he is a hologram. That is enough and we believe it.

THX 1138 is an oppressive film but that does not mean it is not entertaining or at least very engaging. Lucas keeps his emotional distance. When LUH faces the wall and cries, Lucas' camera remains outside the room and so the audience cannot quite empathise in the way a more sentimental close-up would compel them to. Lucas remains similarly cool in the scene where Anakin says farewell to his mother in *The Phantom Menace*. Throughout the *Star Wars* saga, a romantically-inflected music score amplifies emotions but in *THX 1138* there is nothing to guide our emotions. We feel as stranded and lost as the characters in their struggle with important questions. THX asks at one point: "What's wrong with me? What am I to her and she to me? Nothing." This might not be naturalistic dialogue but it is poetic and powerful. The tyranny of naturalism will always be overthrown by strong cinema.

Each scene is more the expression of an idea rather than existing to advance the plot in the classical Hollywood style. The story tells an eternally popular tale of the quest for freedom and self in a very engaging, cinematic and inventive way. Lucas' adherence to the silent film form is evident from the beginning.

As in the *Star Wars* saga, the issue of moving beyond what you know is core to the drama. LUH says to THX, "Don't make trouble. You're going to get us into trouble." Nonetheless, LUH is a strong character, more composed than THX, who is something of an emotional wreck, perhaps because he is more prepared to question and doubt.

THX 1138 contains many ideas, perhaps too many for its scale. Sitting in The White Limbo, THX listens to the ramblings of SEN and much of what is spoken about re-emerges in the *Star Wars* saga. In *THX 1138*, it is the individual who acts on these thoughts rather than the one who sits around talking about them who breaks free. The film does not state what it is that THX is breaking free into. We have no idea of the world beyond, just as THX does not. What is shown in the final image is a supreme picture of nature, space and freedom.

Sound And Vision Keys: Lucas doesn't explain it all. Watching the film it is as though we're dropping in on the world rather than being told a story. Throughout, Lucas cuts away from the main narrative, shows the environment, then cuts back. For example, when THX announces, "I think I'm dying," the shot cuts to hooded figures walking and then returns to THX. Lucas' background as an editor allows him to imply more with disparate images - the hooded figures suggest religion/death/a funeral.

THX 1138, like *The Matrix* and *AI*, shows how the values of human existence clash with those of a speculated future where technology dominates. What more powerful drama/trauma can there be than a threat to humanity? *THX 1138*'s music track contains a harpsichord, a traditional and organic instrument, which contrasts with the overwhelming electronic range of synthesised sounds. Lalo Schifrin's delicate theme for the love scenes between THX and LUH offers a soothing respite from the assault of harsher sounds throughout the film. Lucas also uses the costume design to symbolise the conflict between man and machine. The white outfits worn by the humans contrast with the black leather of the police. Similarly, the people almost disappear when viewed against the white world they live in. The fragility of THX and LUH (and humanity in general) is visually amplified when Lucas places their naked bodies in The White Limbo.

Lucas is always associated with films for young people. In *THX 1138* it is evident that he is capable of a more mature, and more sedate, tone. The scenes where THX and LUH make love are very real and tender.

A menacing string-synthesiser theme emerges over the Warner Brothers logo and the opening credits rise upwards, suggesting the audience's descent into the story. This muted, uninviting opening is as all-encompassing and graphically charged as the openings of *American Graffiti* and *A New Hope*.

There is an appropriate flatness to the graphic design of the film and its creation of spaces, suggesting there is often no room for the characters to breathe. Lucas' camera rarely pans or tilts let alone tracks. The camera is locked off, just as the characters are locked in their world.

Lucas visually impresses his theme of repression and spiritual death through his flat, yet fascinating, images. Once more, form and content are shown to be the same.

For all the film's stillness, its overall visual approach breaks out at the end because the characters also disrupt their norm. Lucas uses the speed suggested by quick cuts and the roar of a sound effect to immerse the viewer in the illusion of speed in the film's end chase. You can easily substitute the tunnel for the Death Star trench and the in-car readouts for the graphics on the control board of X-Wing fighters. The police are unthinking copies, like the stormtroopers of *Star Wars* and the clones who form such a focus for *Star Wars'* second episode. All of Lucas' films celebrate individual thought and action which allow his heroes to break out of a system of established behaviour. In the world of *THX 1138* everybody looks the same. There is a shot in *Attack Of The Clones* where countless identical children sit at monitors. Linking Lucas to the fairy-tale tradition, the children in *THX 1138* learn their lessons through intravenous liquid. In Hans Christian Andersen's story *The Garden Of Paradise* people eat cakes containing information about specific subjects.

Lucas intercuts between film and CCTV/monitor images and this gives the film a different texture. The use of sound and silence amplifies this. There are combinations of choral music and more synthetic sounds. When THX emerges to freedom, he is accompanied by a choral piece of music - a more traditional and human sound, as opposed to the manufactured sounds, drones and 'emotionless' voices of the subterranean world he has emerged from. These motifs and devices repeat on a galactic scale in the *Star Wars* story. Lucas creates a completely believable environment, the "immaculate reality"he describes in so many interviews in later years. As with *American Graffiti*, *A New Hope* and *The Phantom Menace*, Lucas frames much of the drama so that it feels almost wrongly framed, as though he just had time to catch the moment. Consider the dialogue exchange between SEN and THX in SEN's apartment. There are no over-the-shoulder shots. Instead SEN and THX occupy opposite sides of the frame, almost to the point where SEN is barely in shot. In another scene, THX and LUH talk and Lucas frames THX to the edge of the frame again. This is an out-of-balance world, socially and emotionally. During his escape from the underworld, THX's odyssey is shot very much like Luke, Leia and Han's escape on foot from the Death Star. Lucas uses a long lens to capture THX and his hologram pal dashing into frame; it is a highly charged kinetic moment. Like the shot of Han running, with the camera beneath him, tracking ahead, Lucas uses this device to draw us into the moment. The documentary feel of the film is astonishing.

The first few minutes of the film are striking in their creation of a world through the dense layering of sound and image, cut together at a dizzying pace. Watching this sequence you feel almost overwhelmed. Lucas uses purely cinematic tools (sound and vision) to place us in the mindset of his protagonists. Lucas does not resort to dialogue for his emotional effects.

Lucas is very aware of contrasting and juxtaposing shapes and colour. The shaved heads are perfectly round contrasting with the harsh, straight lines of stairways and walls and the blocks of colour and space. This design sense repeats in the *Star Wars* saga. The police cars of *THX 1138* sound like TIE fighters and suggest the podracers and the Millennium Falcon to come. Throughout his career Lucas has emphasised the role of sound and sound design in creating his famous "immaculate reality."

No Lucas film is complete without a chase, giving the audience a kinetic experience that is actually very cinematic. It is rather like taking a theme park ride. Unsurprisingly, throughout his career Lucas' films have been labelled as glorified theme park rides rather than films.

Background: Lucas' aesthetic intention with *THX 1138* was to make a movie that felt as though a documentary camera crew had been sent to the future to follow the story of THX 1138. By using long lenses at certain key points, as he went on to do in all his films as a director, Lucas makes the action feel like it is being captured by an observer who does not want to intrude on the subject. One of the quintessential *Star Wars* images occurs in *The Phantom Menace* where a long lens is used in the scene when our heroes blast their way into the spacecraft hangar, lightsabres blazing and deflecting oncoming laser fire. The long lens makes us feel as though we have just caught the burst of energy in time and the low height of the camera suggests we are crouching, maybe hiding for cover just as someone filming in a war zone trench might.

THX 1138 is an expansion of the short film Lucas made whilst teaching at USC with Navy troops as students and crew. It was financed and released by Warner Brothers but was otherwise a non- Hollywood movie. It was conceived, shot and post-produced in San Francisco, with local crew such as Dave Meyers and Al Kihn, the ace camera operators on the film. It remains Lucas' most obviously non-commercial film as a director.

THX 1138 was Robert Duvall's first major movie, though he had appeared in an early Robert Altman movie, *Countdown*, not long before. All of the locations, with the exception of the TV studio that SEN stumbles across, were found in and around the Bay Area of San Francisco, notably the unopened Bay Area Rapid Transit System. The Laurence Livermore Laboratory was also a key location. Twenty-two locations were used in a 42-day shoot, including the Oakland Coliseum, the San Francisco Pacific Gas and Electric Building and the Marin County Civic Centre. The only fabricated set was THX and SEN's apartment. *THX 1138* was very much filmed as though it were a documentary.

THX 1138 has gone on to enjoy a kind of cult status in part because of the Lucas name. *THX 1138* is dystopian science fiction in the mode of George Orwell's *1984* and Zevgeny Zamayatin's *We*, in contrast to the science fantasy of *Star Wars*.

Verdict: Stark and highly cinematic, *THX 1138* is Lucas' most atypical film as a director and yet contains many of the motifs and themes he has been riffing on ever since. Not as cold a film as reports might indicate. A must-see to get a clearer idea of where *Star Wars* is coming from. 5/5

American Graffiti (1973)

Cast: Richard Dreyfuss (Curt Henderson), Ron Howard (Steve Bolander), Charles Martin Smith (Terry), Paul LeMat (John Milner), Cindy Williams (Laurie Henderson), Candy Clark (Debbie), McKenzie Phillips (Carol), Suzanne Somers (T Bird Blonde), Wolfman Jack (Himself), Bo Hopkins (Lead Pharoh), Harrison Ford (Bob Falfa).

Crew: Director: George Lucas; Screenplay: George Lucas & Willard Huyck & Gloria Katz; Cinematography: Haskell Wexler; Producers: Gary Kurtz & Francis Ford Coppola. Universal Pictures/Lucasfilm Ltd. 110 mins.

Story: A late-summer's night. Four guys meet at Mel's Drive-In and prepare for one last memorable night in a Californian small town. Curt is the intellectual, Steve the class president, Terry the misfit and John the cool car king. Laurie, Steve's girlfriend, joins the guys and the night's adventures begin as the film's narrative rotates between each character's experience of their last night together before leaving home for college. Cruising, meeting girls and realising that times are changing fuel the drama. Curt becomes charmingly obsessed with a dream of a blonde in a Thunderbird. Steve and Laurie's relationship is tested, nearly broken and finally reaffirmed. Terry somehow gets a little cooler and spends a night on the town with a gum-chewing, ballsy girl named Debbie. John cruises town and his cool is seriously tested when he hooks up with a twelve-year-old named Carol. John's evening is made all the more interesting by the arrival of a fellow racer, Bob Falfa, who challenges John to a sunrise race. The movie climaxes with the drag race on Paradise Road. Laurie is almost killed by the race and is reunited with Steve. Terry and John walk off into the sunrise together and Curt heads for college and the wider world. Throughout, the voice of Wolfman Jack acts as chorus to the on-screen action, introducing many classic rock and roll hits from the late 1950s and early 1960s. A series of end notes on-screen detail the fates of the four men. In a very detailed interview about the film back in 1974, Lucas made a comment that stands for all his films, certainly as a director and sometimes as a producer. In a comprehensive interview with Larry Sturhahan in the March 1974 issue of *Filmmakers Newsletter* (pp. 19-27), Lucas stated:

"I'm glad I was a teenager. I don't hang my head and say, 'Well, we were just a bunch of dumb kids then.' We weren't; we were just kids and being a kid is great !"

Themes And Subtext: American Graffiti might, in the really long run, emerge as Lucas' finest hour as a writer and director. The film brims with his essential film-making spirit and we can hope that he will some-day return to making a film or two on this scale again. The film celebrates youth, its energy, confusion and aspiration. It is hard not to feel buoyed up once the film ends. Lucas was knocked out by the letters he received in the wake of the film's hugely successful original release. Teenagers and young adults were saying the film had revived their sense of their younger selves. Like *THX 1138*, *A New Hope* and *The Phantom Menace*, Lucas spins a story about a young man having to move away from the safe and the known. In *American Graffiti* Curt is that character. The name of the aeroplane that whisks him away to a new life at the end of the film is Magic Carpet Airlines. Like Luke Skywalker first seeing Princess Leia in *Star Wars*, when Curt first sees the blonde in the T Bird he is knocked out by her beauty and his quest to somehow speak to her begins. In a 1973 interview, Lucas acknowledged that the girl in the T Bird represents the key to the wider world for Curt. *American Graffiti* ends with Curt looking down from the plane to the highway and the white car driving along below, like a guiding spirit; in a way a more tangible version of The Force.

John Milner's bright yellow deuce coupe gets a starry overhaul in *The Phantom Menace* and becomes a Naboo Starfighter. In *Attack Of The Clones* the vehicles are combined to make the bright yellow speeder that Anakin Skywalker races through the skies of a far-off planet. *American Graffiti* is Lucas' love letter to the late 1950s and early 1960s. It is romantic and nostalgic but carries a truth and accuracy of emotion. Lucas uses the film to create a fantasy realm from the real world, dropping us into that teen culture, never stopping to explain its language and rules.

In an interview with the BBC in 1997 (*Flying Solo: Omnibus Special*), Lucas explained that he likes to see how fast he can tell a story to the point where it might almost become incomprehensible to the audience. *American Graffiti* spins through its multiple storylines, dovetailing them all very neatly in a spectacular finale. Lucas' love of intercutting plotlines is obvious in *American Graffiti* and remained with him throughout his career as both director and producer. In Wolfman Jack, Lucas starts to crystallize and develop his enduring theme of the teacher and the student. Wolfman is really not so far away from Yoda in the *Star Wars* story. Wolfman Jack's advice to a demoralised and confused Curt is: "If the Wolfman were here he'd say 'Get your ass in gear.'" When Luke first realises who Yoda is in *The Empire Strikes Back* his look of recognition equates neatly with Curt's realisation of who the Wolfman is. Curt's discovery and meeting with Wolfman Jack happens at the radio station and carries an eerie and a magical quality to it, rather like Yoda's hut on Dagobah. With certain issues clear in his mind, Curt leaves the Wolfman and embarks on his journey beyond the film.

At the hop, Curt talks with his old teacher who, upon hearing about Curt's doubts about leaving, says: "I wasn't the competitive type. Maybe I got scared. Experience life, have some fun." Curt is the one who makes the break because he has a moment of recognition that things have changed - when he tries to open his old locker at high school he finds that its code has already been changed. As he wrestles with his doubts, Curt's greatest fortune is to be advised during his all-night adventure. Wendy says to Curt: "All the time we were going together you never knew what you were doing." Curt's questioning and anti-authoritarian stance is what frees him. His journey through the night tests his worth so that he is ready to leave by the time the sun comes up. The story begins with Curt suggesting doubts about leaving town to which Steve replies: "We're finally getting out of this turkey town and you want to crawl back into your cell, right? You want to end up like John? You just can't stay seventeen forever." At the end of the film, Curt goes and Steve stays in town.

If Curt is Luke Skywalker in his yearning for more then John Milner is the equivalent of Han in his weird yearning for less. There is a neat melancholy to John too when he reminisces about times gone by: "It was really somethin'." It is evident from his facial expression that he hates the idea of his friends leaving town. Later in the film John takes the young Carol for a walk through an old car yard and he recalls the fast times and history of the valley. John is clearly a little older than the other guys but will not admit to it. His most plaintive reflection is when he states that "Rock 'n' roll's been goin' downhill ever since Buddy Holly died." As the film's end note makes clear, he pays the price for not accepting that things change and life moves on. Even sadder still is that Terry considers John such a role model. Terry is a successor to the hologram in *THX 1138* and a precursor to the comic sidekick role of Jar-Jar Binks. Like Han, though, John Milner has the stereotypical heart of gold. He is very much a cowboy and is ultimately a big brother/guardian figure for Carol and Terry. John has the young punk quality of James Dean. In talking about his casting of Anakin Skywalker for *Attack Of The Clones*, Lucas has referred to capturing something of a James Dean spirit in the character.

Like all good teen movies *American Graffiti* ends on a note of apocalypse as the car flips and explodes on Paradise Road. You can only wonder if this event scares Steve into not leaving town. It certainly wakes him up to his love for Laurie. Things do go wrong and our relationships are what makes it easier to cope. Steve and Laurie cling to one another at the roadside.

In all his films, Lucas lays sequences out as little riffs on very specific and simple ideas. All the women in *American Grafitti* are very strong; a Lucas film trait. Laurie Henderson looks very much like Princess Leia albeit in sneakers and a tartan miniskirt. Terry's goofy, clumsy faithfulness to the cool John Milner predates Jar-Jar Binks' faithfulness to the cool Jedi Knights he finds himself in tow with. *American Graffiti* is very much a fantasy too and Lucas does not stop to explain any references or words that are particular to that world. When Terry talks about Steve's car at the beginning of the film you either get the references or you don't.

Sound And Vision Keys: As with all Lucas films what we hear is as significant as what we see. For a nuanced and engaging reflection on sound in film check out Walter Murch's rewarding essay 'Sound Design: The Dancing Shadow' in *Projections 4* (Faber and Faber 1995, pp. 237-251).

American Graffiti begins with the sound of a radio tuning in. In this film the radio and music are a binding force that ties the community together, serving as commentary on the drama and dilemma unfolding in the lives of the characters. The film bursts with colour, even down to the coronas around the street lamps. The whole world glows with neon and brightly-coloured cars generating a kind of heightened reality. From the first image - a wide shot of Mel's Diner - the film is bright. Lucas' graphic sense understands the emotional impact of colours above and beyond the emotional impact of dialogue and drama. His economical direction establishes characters through their posture and gesture before we hear a word they say. Steve leans nonchalantly on his car, Terry clumsily crashes into a drinks machine on his scooter and Curt kicks with frustration at his Volkswagen. The costumes (by Aggie Guerard Rogers who reprised her role on *Return Of The Jedi*) say as much too: Curt's checked, jumble of colours (the test card as Haskell Wexler called it on location); Steve's easygoing, almost bland blue shirt; Terry's gauche pink shirt; and John's cool and classic white T-shirt and jeans. The girls are similarly defined: Laurie's tartan miniskirt and cardigan suggest an iconic high-school image; Debbie is a little more elaborate and dressed for the night; Carol is decked out in T-shirt and jeans and way too young for a night on the town anyway. In Lucas' re-release of the film in 1998 ILM added a dazzling sunset sky behind the diner at the beginning of the film to balance with the sunrise at the end. Throughout the film Lucas' camera remains at a distance from the action, lending the story a similar documentary quality to *THX 1138*. Check out the early scene as 'Sixteen Candles' plays on the soundtrack and Lucas' camera picks out the girls on rollerskates serving burgers. The cutaways to shots of the cars racing up and down the main drag work in the same way. Lucas quietly immerses you in his world, just as he immerses you in the worlds of *Star Wars*. For Lucas, films serve as artefacts of a moment in time, capturing the concerns and dreams of an age.

Background: Accounts of the production of *American Graffiti* are as entertaining as the film itself. There is a David and Goliath aspect to the film's production in the way that Lucas and Coppola dealt with the studio. Lucas was partly prompted to develop the film when Coppola challenged him to create something warm in opposition to the starker palette of *THX 1138*. Lucas had never considered himself a writer but he knew aware that the challenge was to create sympathetic characters that the audience could relate to. It was also his first attempt at comedy. Lucas crafted a treatment which got interest from Universal Pictures. He called upon his old USC pals, writers Willard Huyck and Gloria Katz to flesh out the material when another writer had failed to create a draft that met Lucas' expectations. The rewrite preserved Lucas' structure and the majority of his characterisations. Huyck and Katz's major contribution was the dialogue and building up the character of Steve. In 1972, Lucas was still a relative unknown in Hollywood, although the reasonably positive critical reception for *THX 1138* proved Lucas could intrigue an audience with a concept and its realisation. Coppola served as executive producer. He was fresh from his success on *The Godfather* so his name suddenly had a certain market value. The budget of $777,777.77 was very low given the percentage paid to secure rights to 45 rock 'n' roll classics. Lucas filmed for 28 nights, starting on 26 June 1972, initially in San Rafael, Northern California, and soon after in Petaluma when San Rafael complained about filming affecting trade. The script was 140 pages long. Some nights Lucas and his crew managed thirty set-ups. The initial cut of the film was about 140 minutes and Lucas then spent almost a year refining the cut to bring it to within two hours. Lucas said that the original cut really worked and the trick was to keep that effectiveness despite having to lose so much. Marcia Lucas edited the film with veteran Verna Fields, who went on to edit *Jaws* (1975) for Steven Spielberg. When *American Graffiti* was screened at a San Francisco cinema on Sunday morning in the summer of 1973 the audience loved the film. The Universal Studio executives did not, saying that it might find a place as a TV movie. Coppola became enraged, telling the suits they should be grateful that Lucas had come in on budget and time and created a terrific film. Lucas was apparently very quiet as Coppola assumed the role of the protective and confident producer, offering to buy the film off Universal and distribute it himself. The film was released on 1 August 1973. Spielberg said: "I thought and still do to this day, I just thought *American Graffiti* was the best American film I'd seen."(Interview with Simon Hattenstone, p. 4, *The Guardian*, 11 September 1998.)

American Graffiti was the most profitable film Hollywood had ever funded - apparently for every $1 invested Universal Studios made back

$50. The film eventually pulled in $117 million at the box office. It was included in the first 25 films selected for America's National Film Registry, an archive that preserves films for posterity. If further proof were needed of the film's pop culture standing you can now buy toy models of the cars featured in the film standing against a little cardboard background of Mel's Drive-In.

With the film a hit, Lucas finally moved towards his long-cherished independence and began work in earnest on his space fantasy project, at the time called *The Star Wars*. Lucas turned down other offers of movies, such as *Lucky Lady*, to work on developing the *Star Wars* script. His integrity and commitment to his work reaped its own reward and has made him a role model for independent film-makers.

Verdict: Lucas does on film for American teen culture in the early 1960s what the great Brian Wilson and The Beach Boys did in music. Lucas makes it iconic and highly appealing. *American Graffiti* is a real summertime movie. Nostalgic with traces of doubt and hesitation amidst the energy. 5/5

Star Wars: Episode IV: A New Hope (1977)

Cast: Mark Hamill (Luke Skywalker), Harrison Ford (Han Solo), Carrie Fisher (Princess Leia), Sir Alec Guinness (Obi-Wan Kenobi), Peter Mayhew (Chewbacca), Anthony Daniels (C-3PO), Kenny Baker (R2-D2), Peter Cushing (Grand Moff Tarkin), Phil Brown (Uncle Owen), Shelagh Fraser (Aunt Beru).

Crew: Writer/Director: George Lucas; Producer: Gary Kurtz; Music: John Williams; Production Designer: John Barry; Director of Photography: Gil Taylor; Special Visual Effects: Industrial Light and Magic; Editor: Marcia Lucas. Twentieth Century-Fox/Lucasfilm Ltd. 121 mins.

Story: A fast and furious space chase and shoot-out take place above a sandy planet. A young, brave Princess is taken prisoner by the villainous Darth Vader, agent of the Empire in the ongoing struggle between the Imperial forces and the plucky Rebel Alliance fighting for freedom from tyranny. Princess Leia is taken to the Death Star. In the melee, two bungling droids, fussy C-3PO and sparky R2-D2, escape capture and crash-land on the remote desert planet of Tatooine. The droids are picked up by scrap merchants and then bought by a desert farmer named Owen Lars. Living with Owen is his nephew (apparently), Luke Skywalker. Luke is a young man who yearns for a bigger life and dreams of someday joining the rebellion against the Empire. Luke soon discovers that R2-D2 carries a message from Leia in which she pleads for the help of a man named Obi-Wan (Ben) Kenobi. On board the Death Star, Leia is interrogated about the Rebel Alliance and even sees her home world of Alderaan destroyed by the Empire. Soon enough Luke meets Kenobi, an aging ex-Jedi Knight living in the wastes of Tatooine. Kenobi heeds the call for help and eventually convinces Luke to join him. Looking for a transport off Tatooine, Luke and Ben meet up with cocky space ace, Han Solo, and his co-pilot Chewbacca. They head for the stars, Solo more interested in his payment than in any kind of rescue. Solo's ship is ensnared by the Death Star. Inside, Han and Luke try to rescue Leia whilst Kenobi heads off for a confrontation with his old nemesis Darth Vader. With Leia rescued, our heroes go to the planet Yavin, next in line for Death Star destruction. Luke pilots one of the X-Wing fighters as the Rebel forces launch an assault on the Death Star. Luke is the hero of the hour as the Death Star is destroyed, Vader's ship spiralling uncontrollably out into space. Our heroes are reunited and their victory against the odds celebrated.

Themes And Subtext: What more can be written about this defining movie? It is a slightly odd feeling to be writing about a film that has been a part of this writer's life from day one. The film's images, dialogue, pacing, music and tone have truly become part of the popular culture. The film's fairy-tale aspect is not just in its character types and situations but the pace at which the story is told. In his book *Six Walks In The Fictional Woods*, literary theorist and writer Umberto Eco comments that fairy tale narratives do not linger, they tell what you need to know and move on. In a way it is hard to imagine life without *A New Hope*. It will probably always stand as Lucas' most famous film, a near-perfect distillation of his preoccupations and craft. It is a simple story, classically American, rendered through an application of groundbreaking technology and surefire storytelling. And whilst so many love it, so many loathe it too, seeing it as the curse of narrative mainstream American cinema. The film combines genre forms, references to old movies, comic books, old TV serials and myths and legends. For some this is the height of invention. For others it is the height of mediocrity and a second-rate kind of creativity that is seen as the start of an irreversible decline on Lucas' part - he is seen by some as simply a rehasher of a disparate array of stories to create his own material aimed squarely at young people and older people who should know better. Maybe this is more a reflection on the standing of adventure stories and fantasy. Lucas is a postmodern film-maker, widely and openly referencing other stories, though that is only evident if you know the other stories. Alternatively, Lucas can be seen as serving up the most traditional of stories in a way which is accessible and speaks especially powerfully to the young, offering them ideas about the world in an easily digested form. Lucas' films have always contained a range of references to ideas and social issues.

A New Hope has a simple range of emotions that shine with a certain innocence. *The Phantom Menace* arguably has a richer emotional palette and deals with a wider range of issues, from political manoeuvering to ecological concerns, but lacks *A New Hope*'s all-out freewheeling spirit and human spontaneity. Just think about Luke's enthusiasm when he first sees Leia: "Who is she? She's beautiful."

Luke Skywalker is the character the audience associate most strongly with as he is drawn into worlds beyond his normal life. Like Curt Henderson, Luke longs to live big. When Luke meets C-3PO and R2-D2 his description of his home planet is: "If there's a bright centre to the universe, you're on the planet that it's farthest from."

Key to the success of *A New Hope*, beyond the bright lights and noise, is the concept of The Force. Ben Kenobi describes it to Luke as being, "an energy field that binds the galaxy together." The concept gets much more screen time in *The Empire Strikes Back*. *A New Hope* demonstrated that by tuning into The Force (feeling, intuition, community) all things are possible and anybody can do it with commitment and focus.

The film's colour schemes also hold huge appeal in a more subconscious way. If you asked most *Star Wars* fans to associate a colour with *A New Hope* it would be the yellow of the sands. Lucas has acknowledged his colour scheme plan, evidence of his visual sense. The film goes from the white interior of the Blockade Runner (recalling *THX 1138*) to the warm, friendly sands of Tatooine to the harsh, hard-lined, dark interior of the Death Star before finally returning to the forests and stone of Yavin for the celebration scene.

Lucas does not write complicated characters. Instead they are immediately readable and serve as vessels to hold certain ideas. As such they have an archetypal quality although each actor gives the characters inflection and individuality. One of the great strengths of the film is its performances. When you watch the film a second time you realise how much of it is effectively about teenagers bickering as they save the galaxy. Luke's journey away from his small world remains Lucas' boldest statement of the need to grab your surfboard and ride the wave. Even Kenobi says warmly to Luke during a very basic Force training session: "…you've taken your first step into a larger world." Kenobi is very much Wolfman Jack without the howls, wielding a lightsabre rather than a Popsicle.

The film's production design and graphic sense reaffirms the themes of the film. Obi-Wan's looks and gazes are as important as what he says with dialogue. When Leia appears in the hologram, his silent response is heavy with an unspoken recognition. It is a human moment. There is no spectacle, no visual effects, just a face. Lucas never loses sight of the human root of the fantasy, as the dinner table sequence demonstrates. The Rebels are ramshackle and their ships battered and almost home-grown. They have the feeling of being not much more than supped-up bicycles or racing cars. The Imperial forces are defined by straight lines and dark colours, contrasting with the bright orange of the Rebel fly-suits and the forest greens of their base on Yavin.

Right up until 1999, *A New Hope* always seemed expansive in its settings. Rather amusingly, when put up against Lucas' fourth film as a director, *The Phantom Menace*, the original comes across charmingly poky and small.

Lucas' motif of appearances being deceptive is played out right across the *Star Wars* saga. In *A New Hope* Obi-Wan might be a hermit and a "crazy old wizard" to those who don't understand, but to those who do he is a great Jedi Knight. The Millennium Falcon might be "a heap of junk" but when needed the ship can get you where you need to go. Solo speaks to the ship like a car fanatic might to their car. John Milner's spirit is as much present in *Star Wars* as the spirit of The Force.

Compassion is a key theme that Lucas starts to express in *A New Hope*. Leia has a hard time with Han Solo partly because Solo seems unable to commit to a cause larger than himself. "Your friend is quite a mercenary. I wonder if he really cares about anything. Or anyone," Leia comments to Luke about Han. "I care," says Luke, without irony. By the close of the film, Solo (the name says it all) will have demonstrated his commitment to the cause by piloting the Millennium Falcon into the Death Star's orbit to help Luke. In the films that follow *A New Hope*, Solo matures in his relationships with Luke, Leia and the larger cause. He becomes Luke's older brother.

The film initiates the saga's wider expression of the tension between the commitments of day-to-day living and the call of a wider issue. When Obi-Wan wants to go to find Leia, Luke balks: "I've got to get home. It's late. I'm in for it as it is. I can't get involved… It's all such a long way from here." When Luke does embark on his journey, the first stop is the cantina which embodies the diversity and intrigue of the world outside his home.

A New Hope expresses the conflict between following received orders and going your own way. The Emprie is built on hierarchy and fear. Its angular, rigid forms and grey colours reinforce this. In contrast, the association of Luke with the golden glow of the desert and then of the Rebels' forest hideaway on Yavin equates the natural world with positive characters. The Rebels' ships lack clean lines; they seem more like toys, friendlier with colourful insignia.

The Force promotes instinctive behaviour that disconnects from the social order (individualism). One of the great American preoccupations is with the freedom of the individual. This is both a positive and a negative power. Luke represents the balance between individual needs and those of his world. Anakin Skywalker, however, is driven by selfish individualism. The film's heroes are all sorts of shapes and sizes. There is nothing uniform about them. Like so many Westerns, Lucas celebrates diverse individuals coming together.

The *Star Wars* saga reveals itself to be one huge story about growing up, fuelling its fireworks and pizzazz with concerns about loyalty, family, betrayal, trust, romantic and compassionate love, and community. Lucas' repetitions and cycles of events begin to accumulate in effect. Watching *The Phantom Menace* followed by *A New Hope* reveals the true extent of Obi-Wan's sadness. We see him as a young and vibrant Jedi in *The Phantom Menace* and then as an old man in *A New Hope*. In *A New Hope* it is the Rebels who win, partly because of their warmth and unity. In the *Star Wars* movies that followed, the best moments were often the smallest, the least visually spectacular. In *A New Hope* the defining image is of Luke gazing at the setting suns as John Williams' score tenderly accentuates the emotion of loneliness and the sense of something larger at work in Skywalker's life. *Star Wars* celebrates youthful energy and promise as it outwits the adult world of the Empire with all its resources and organisation.

Sound And Vision Keys: Everything in a film frame should count for something. Lucas creates a completely believable world, a 'used universe' design that John Barry so brilliantly executed. Lucas' silent movie aesthetic is everywhere in *Star Wars*. The last few minutes are purely sound and image. Throughout the film, Lucas' attachment to the films of Akira Kurosawa is evident (the 'wipes' from one scene to another, and more than one tip of the hat to *The Hidden Fortress*). Lucas uses his pastiche of cinematic, historical and literary forms as a shorthand for the audience. For children watching, the film simply works as an entity because their knowledge of other stories is less extensive. Some of the images and designs are elemental and universal in their associations. When we see someone in a hood and cloak we immediately connect them with something more spiritual. Luke's poncho recalls the Western. Han Solo's sleeveless waistcoat and laser pistol on the hip recall countless images of the American cowboy. The wall lights of the Death Star have a Japanese aspect to them. Watch Kurosawa's *Throne Of Blood* and note the round-ended elongated shapes on the wall in an early scene. For all of the visual intensity, none of the environments overshadow the drama being played out in and around them. The colour schemes, location and architecture enhance and symbolise the human drama.

Lucas' graphic sense is apparent from the film's first image of the triangular Star Destroyer. Lucas' brilliant editing sense culminates in the Death Star attack but is especially effective when stormtroopers fire at the Millennium Falcon in Tatooine.

The documentary style once again comes into play throughout. Lucas' zooms in on C-3PO and R2-D2 when we first see them in that immense shot on Tatooine. It is as though we have just sighted them rather like wildlife. Look at Lucas' hand-held shots of the Jawas in the rocks or the scene where Luke and his pals race for the Falcon as Kenobi duels with Darth Vader. When Uncle Owen and Luke first meet the droids and Jawas it is shot with a long lens so that the audience feels like an observer just across the way and that the actors are not performing for the camera. This is a cinematic form of characterisation. Luke runs across the sand whilst his gruff uncle shambles along. *Star Wars* uses storytelling of believable action rather than complex psychology.

John Williams' score was partly responsible for the revival of symphonic film scoring in the late 1970s. The form endures today. As Williams and many others have noted, the score employs a musical motif for each character which can be duly integrated into the more 'generic' passages. *A New Hope* redefined a certain kind of Hollywood film and also initiated a profound development in the application of optical effects in films. Three documentary-flavoured shots stand out: the first image of Luke Skywalker as he runs towards the sandcrawler; Han Solo blasting stormtroopers just before rocketing out of Mos Eisley; and also Luke and Leia's swing across the chasm. As in *American Grafitti*, Lucas' camera rarely pans, tracks or tilts. Instead motion is created through the editing.

Background: Lucas had always been intrigued by the serials made in the 1930s and 1940s, and was looking for a new way to revise their forms and aesthetics to forge a new mythology for young people. Lucas began developing ideas for the project in the early 1970s, and appears to have begun seriously considering what to do with his basic concept by 1972, when *American Graffiti* was in production. After the release of *American Graffiti*, Lucas accumulated source and reference materials to help him create a story that would be familiar and yet very different. For all his wild imaginings, Lucas was acutely aware of the limitations of special effects technology at that time. As Lucas developed his synopsis, the story became unwieldy and formed the root of two trilogies. With so much developed story, Lucas had to focus on the most achievable and affordable aspect of the story. Inevitably, ideas and narrative threads had to be discarded, but the phenomenal success of the first film has meant that many of these have eventually made it to the screen. For example, one of Lucas' original synopses introduces Annikin Starkiller, his brother Kane and their father Deak. Deak is killed by a Sith warrior and Kane rescues Annikin from the same threat. This was the root of the Darth Maul fight scene on the desert planet in *The Phantom Menace*. Also, Luke Skywalker was originally called Luke Starkiller and the name was changed just before shooting began.

Lucas invested some of the profits from *American Graffiti* into the development of *The Star Wars* as it was originally titled. He established Industrial Light and Magic to begin developing not only effects and designs but new technology to realise the effects. John Dykstra created the Dykstraflex camera capable of multiple computer-controlled passes of a model. To encourage studio interest, Lucas brought in Ralph McQuarrie to provide character designs and production paintings of key scenes and moments in the envisioned film. McQuarrie had been an illustrator at NASA and Boeing amongst others and successfully crystallised Lucas' fusion of the hi tech with the fantastic and organic. An early McQuarrie painting features stormtroopers with shields and one wielding a lightsabre. The Millennium Falcon once looked very much like the maroon Jedi ship that arrives at the start of *The Phantom Menace*.

In July 1987, *Starlog* magazine ran a special issue devoted to *Star Wars* on its tenth anniversary. Journalists Randy and Jean-Marc Lofficier provided a very comprehensive guide to the development of the scripts that became *Star Wars*. Lucas ultimately had too big a story for one film and so cut it into sections which roughly became the sequels and episodes one, two and three. Another fascinating read is Laurent Bouzereau's *Star Wars: The Annotated Screenplays* which features the scripts for *Star Wars*, *The Empire Strikes Back* and *Return Of The Jedi*, supplemented by new interviews with Lucas, Ralph McQuarrie, Joe Johnston, Irvin Kershner, Lawrence Kasdan and others about their work and the issues the films were designed to articulate. Suffice to say, Lucas wrote numerous storylines and scripts and it is fascinating to see how ideas and characters come, go, return and mutate as Lucas synthesised and reinvented influences from the history of literature, comic books and old movies. At one point, Han Solo was an alien and at another he was black. Luke and Leia could have been portrayed by actors of short height. Leia was almost Eurasian and Toshiro Mifune was considered for Obi-Wan Kenobi. Yet, when the film was released there was concern from some that the film was not racially diverse and that it propagated fascist ethics. In Lucas' universe many of the morally monstrous characters are creatures. In 1999, Robert Hughes wrote a scathing review of *The Phantom Menace* which claimed the same. It was a thunderous and well-written article.

Lucas' raison d'être for *Star Wars* was to provide young people with a new fairy tale and maybe even a sense of basic morality. Over the years his story has become a legitimate part of American expression as *The Adventures Of Huckleberry Finn* and *The Wizard Of Oz*. L Frank Baum created many stories in his world of Oz which, like *Star Wars*, is a bold fantasy very clearly rooted in real emotional experience.

Lucas had an arduous task selling *Star Wars* to the studios and eventually Twentieth Century-Fox picked it up with Alan Ladd Jr. having absolute faith in Lucas' ability to deliver it from the beginning. Lucas began preparing the film in earnest in 1975. Casting was huge and followed the same pattern as for *American Graffiti* - auditioning hundreds and hundreds of young actors. Lucas eventually whittled the potential actors for Han, Luke and Leia down to several trios. Famously, Sylvester Stallone and Christopher Walken might have been Han Solos. Harrison Ford was kind of cast by accident. He was working as a carpenter at the building where the auditions were being held. When Lucas needed someone to read lines opposite a hopeful Luke or Leia he asked Ford to step in. Ford's reluctance and weariness won through and he was cast as Han.

The film was shot on location in Tunisia, Death Valley, Guatemala and at Elstree Studios in north London. Lucas' cinematographer was Gil Taylor whose credits included *Dr Strangelove* and *A Hard Day's Night*. Taylor's lighting plan focused on creating an even light across the sets so that Lucas could film wherever he wanted. 7,000 photoflood lamps were fixed behind the walls of the Death Star.

Originally scheduled for Christmas 1976 release, it became apparent the film would not make that deadline and so May 1977 was the new delivery date. Many of Lucas' movie-making pals were invited to his home just north of San Francisco for a screening of the film. Brian De Palma was in attendance and recalls that he was a little sceptical of the film. Steven Spielberg said that he thought the film would be a massive hit. Despite the enthusiasm of Spielberg and film critic and screenwriter Jay Cocks, Lucas felt pessimistic. In December 1976 theatres ran a very simple teaser poster in white block capitals on a black background simply reading: "A long time ago in a galaxy far, far away…" Some audiences laughed at the trailer. The film was so successful that it was re-released in 1978 - in pre-video days the only way to revisit a film was by listening to its soundtrack.

Lucas sometimes dismissed *Star Wars*' success as being down to people enjoying "dumb movies" but his feeling had shifted by the early 1990s. Whilst he had always hoped it would connect with young people especially, he never expected it to do so to the degree it did. The mistakes and inadequacies he saw in the material perhaps stopped him enjoying the full and positive impact the movie was having on so many. By 1991, *Star Wars* experienced something of a revival which may have showed Lucas that his story was more than just a diversion, a side-show. By the end of 1994 Lucas was at work crafting the first three episodes of the story.

The Verdict: Lucas' cinematic legacy. Slower than some might recall, the action scenes remain all-time classics and the film has an old swashbuckling quality to it. The ultimate bubblegum movie. It feels less like a film and more like a ride, proving Lucas' skill at immersing us in a universe through which the movie carries us. 5/5

Star Wars: Episode I: The Phantom Menace (1999)

Cast: Liam Neeson (Qui-Gon Jinn), Ewan McGregor (Obi-Wan Kenobi), Natalie Portman (Queen Padmé Amidala), Ian McDiarmid (Senator Palpatine), Anthony Daniels (C-3PO), Kenny Baker (R2-D2), Frank Oz (Yoda), Ahmed Best (Jar-Jar Binks), Brian Blessed (Boss Nass), Hugh Quarshie (Captain Panaka), Terrence Stamp (Chancellor Valorum), Ray Park (Darth Maul), Ralph Brown (Ric Olie).

Crew: Writer/Director: George Lucas; Producer: Rick McCallum; Director of Photography: David Tattersall; Special Visual Effects: Industrial Light and Magic; ILM Supervisors: John Knoll & Rob Coleman & Dennis Muren; Production Designer: Gavin Bouquet; Music: John Williams; Costume: Trisha Biggar; Design: Doug Chiang & Ian McCaig. Twentieth Century-Fox. 125 mins.

Story: The peaceful planet of Naboo is blockaded by the Trade Federation as part of larger deception on the part of an emerging politician seeking to control the galaxy. Two Jedi Knights, Qui-Gon Jinn and Obi-Wan Kenobi, are dispatched to negotiate a treaty but chaos ensues. Naboo is soon under siege and young Queen Padmé Amidala taken prisoner. Taking cover from the Trade Federation on Naboo, Qui-Gon Jinn and Obi-Wan Kenobi enlist the help of a hapless creature named Jar-Jar Binks, who gets them to the Queen's castle. In an effort to rescue Queen Amidala, they find themselves on the small planet of Tatooine. The Jedi are pursued by a Sith Jedi, Darth Maul, under the orders of Darth Sidious. The Jedi cross paths with a bright young boy named Anakin Skywalker within whom Qui-Gon Jinn recognises great potential. Anakin's mother gives the Jedi permission to take Anakin away for training as a Jedi. The Jedi go to the Jedi Council at Coruscant to present Anakin as the Chosen One. The Council are reluctant. The Trade Federation continue their invasion of Naboo and Senator Palpatine, representing Naboo, manoeuvres himself into position as Chancellor. Returning to Naboo our heroes enlist the support of the subterranean Gungan race to fight the army of Battle Droids and tanks. Using primitive but effective weaponry, our heroes defeat the Trade Federation on land and in space, with the significant intervention of Anakin, whilst the Jedi confront Darth Maul in a lethal three-way lightsabre duel. Anakin is accepted by the Jedi Council as a new student and Naboo celebrate their freedom.

Themes And Subtext: When we first meet Obi-Wan Kenobi and his teacher Qui-Gon Jinn, Obi-Wan comments: "I have a bad feeling about this." Qui-Gon replies: "Don't centre on your anxieties, Obi-Wan." Lucas' dialogue has frequently been described as tin ear but a case can be made for its non-naturalistic flow enhancing the fantasy. The dialogue functions as a chorus, returning us to the very austere and emblematic dialogue of *THX 1138* which comments on what we are seeing rather than advancing it. This hyper-real language is never more apparent than when Qui-Gon talks to Jar-Jar Binks of "the sound of a thousand terrible things headed this way." Obi-Wan Kenobi (he is not called Ben at this stage) has the clean-cut look of eager youth whilst Qui-Gon's long hair speaks of a man unconcerned with vanity. Where the overriding theme of *A New Hope* was getting out into the world and making your mark, *The Phantom Menace* is more inclined to issues of community and guardianship. Lucas continues to spotlight the interface between humans and machines, always with the suggestion that too much reliance on the technological is not the best way to go. In spring 1994, Lucas received an honorary degree from USC and in his acceptance speech reflected on the idea of symbiosis. Clearly he was anticipating one of the ways in which he frames the idea of community in the film. The Gungans and Naboo people must unite, using the best of what they have to offer in order to protect their home. Qui-Gon Jinn makes a more explicit reference to this when talking with Anakin on the landing platform on Coruscant when he discusses the midichlorian count in Anakin's blood supply.

The film has far less of the 'gee whiz' feeling about it than *A New Hope* did. This first episode is deliberately paced, taking on board a wide range of issues and emotions. The funeral pyre scene is charged with doubt and uncertainty and this tempers the end celebrations. The story's young phantom menace is standing beside Yoda and Obi-Wan, dressed as a Jedi student, his hair shorn, with a single braid hanging down. Lucas has designed the story as a stand-alone piece but also as an introduction to the saga.

Just as Ben instructed Luke to concentrate in *A New Hope* and as Yoda elaborated in *The Empire Strikes Back*, so too Anakin is introduced to the idea of focus by Qui-Gon. Qui-Gon is another in Lucas' long line of father figures looking after the well-being of someone younger.

The Jedi represent quiet assurance and confidence, right down to the sure footedness of their walk. When they finally confront Darth Maul, look how measured and contained their movement is. Maul paces edgily whilst Qui-Gon kneels and meditates.

To promote *The Phantom Menace*, Lucasfilm produced several 'tone poem' commercials, a combination of images from the films with a key character narrating a piece of blank verse poetry over them - a little like galactic haiku. The slightly abstract approach of the ads brought Lucas full circle in stylistic terms and encapsulated the various central themes of the film in a very effective way. The poems include statements which would not have been out of place in the film itself, particularly in Anakin's *One Dream* 'tone poem.'

Lucas' ecological motif runs through the film. When the Trade Federation H-shaped ships land in the forest Lucas acknowledges and implicitly critiques deforestation. When Qui-Gon runs from the huge machines the statement is plainer still as trees are felled and countless tiny animals flee for cover. When Jar-Jar arrives on Tatooine he even says "the sun doin' murder to my skin." This intrusion of technology and industry is also referenced when the Queen's ship returns to Naboo towards the end of the film. Watch as the flock of birds rise from the tree canopies. The Gungan race are attuned to nature and have clearly built an impressive culture with it. There is nothing primitive about them at all, counter to Obi-Wan's initial scepticism (racism) towards Jar-Jar Binks which finally gives way when Obi-Wan says to Jar-Jar: "You (the Gungans) and the Naboo form a symbiant circle." Jar-Jar is the unwitting lucky charm of the adventure. Lucas' film is fuelled by a declaration of peace and understanding. At the end of the film the very last word to be spoken is "Peace." Qui-Gon remains open-minded and always ready to embrace the potential of those he meets. He is a humanist. Boss Nass the Gungan leader acknowledges the arrogance of the human Naboo race before forming an alliance with them against the Mekaneeks (mechanics).

Perhaps the most controversial aspect of the film was the character of Jar-Jar Binks who some saw as an unthinking throwback to racial stereotypes of old and as a source of sometimes lazy humour. Jar-Jar's role as a comic character was seen as somehow destroying *Star Wars'* sense of seriousness. To some it was like putting Roger Rabbit into space. Jar-Jar's noise and frantic energy contrast and throw into relief the calm and focus of the Jedi and ultimately each way is shown to be effective by the end of the story. In fact, Binks' broad comedy hi-jinks successfully counterpoint the film's predominantly serious tone. It is a less zestful film than many expected. In story terms he serves the same kind of role as Sancho Panza in *Don Quixote*, where Panza is the comic foil to a knight, deflating often overly pompous behaviour. Or like Stan Laurel does to Oliver Hardy. Binks is very much a trickster figure from the mythologies of the world who counterpoints the noble intentions and self-importance of humans. Lucas also makes a point about Binks without recourse to dialogue. Jar-Jar is a clumsy, insecure and permanently panic-stricken character away from home in the big bad world. It is these apparently negative traits which serve him best as the final battle shows. For some, though, Jar-Jar's antics throw the film's 'seriousness' off balance.

Yoda sums up the entire saga to come when he says: "Fear leads to anger. Anger leads to hate. Hate leads to suffering."

Sound And Vision Keys: At the beginning, in the first of many continuations of the *Star Wars* tradition, the camera tilts down from a starry sky after the exposition has crawled into infinity. A starship approaches from the left of the frame and Lucas' camera pans right with it. Gone are the days of a cut as the ship exits the frame and then a cut to the ship reentering the frame from behind the camera.

The design of *The Phantom Menace* has a strong Oriental quality to it but that even extends to the kinds of cups Qui-Gon and Obi-Wan drink from as they sit at the table waiting to meet with the Trade Federation. The blue and grey environment contrasts with warm browns and tans of the Jedi clothes, and with the vibrantly bright and colourful lightsabres.

The Phantom Menace expanded the scale of the *Star Wars* environment, showing just how impressionistic the various environments in Episodes IV, V and VI were. Lucas pursues his concept of an "immaculate reality" in the creation of other worlds. The three-way finale jumps with ease between live action and what is effectively a cartoon (the battle on the Naboo plains). Only the realism of the animation makes us forget how the events have been created. For some though, the film was too much animation and not enough realism.

In *The Phantom Menace*, Lucas' camera moves with fluidity and expanse, immersing us in the highly-detailed worlds, each of which has very obvious real-world reference points. The film is heavy with ideas and references rather like *THX 1138*.

Lucas' documentary aesthetic continues. When we first see the Naboo palace, the camera glides high above it as though the shot has been grabbed from a helicopter. The same technique is used for the opening master shot of the stadium for the pod race. To enhance the sense of reality, Lucas packs out each frame with activity in the background and foreground. The main characters are surrounded by creatures, aliens, sights, sounds, smells, objects, machines. Just watch the sequence when Qui-Gon, Amidala, Jar-Jar and R2-D2 enter Mos Espa.

Scale is important in the *Star Wars* world. Yoda is the smallest member of the Jedi Council but also the most powerful. Anakin Skywalker is a nine-year-old boy from a backwater planet yet he is labelled The Chosen One who will restore order to the galaxy. Darth Sidious is a frail, hooded man of immense corruption and influence. The Naboo Starfighters, small and bright like toys, go up against the mammoth machine of the Trade Federation. The Gungan warriors overcome the Trade Federation army. In Lucas' world, small always wins out over big.

As with Princess Leia, Lucas creates a strongwilled, though less 'streetwise,' female protagonist in Amidala. Amidala is another of Lucas' strong women: Marion Ravenwood in *Raiders Of The Lost Ark*, Laurie in *American Grafitti*, Sorsha in *Willow* and LUH in *THX 1138*.

The most emotional moments in *The Phantom Menace* are the closeups: Anakin saying goodbye to his mother, Obi-Wan saying goodbye to Qui-Gon Jinn. This is a film where a look is worth far more than dialogue - think about the end of the film at Qui-Gon's funeral and the series of glances that are exchanged by those around the funeral pyre. The entire film is underlined by a sense of numb inevitability. We know where Anakin Skywalker is headed and this gives the story a muted sense of resignation. Interestingly, Anakin's first appearance in the film is a very understated moment, in contrast to Luke Skywalker's appearance in *A New Hope*. But then to the characters in the story Anakin is not special at all when he first appears. Through the film, Lucas strives to create role models. The Jedi are calm, Anakin is confident, Padmé is strong and committed.

"Are you an angel?"Anakin asks Padmé soon after meeting her, hinting at the romance to come many years later. "Someday I'm going to fly away from this place," Anakin states assuredly. He has the same yearning as Luke and his openness towards people is a real strength. Lucas' interest in issues of emotional intelligence fuels this film. In the street confrontation with Sebulba the scene becomes a little expression about whether you react with anger or calm to confrontation. On the larger scale, this informs the Jedi/Sith/Skywalker drama. The Sith are driven by revenge.

In 1983 Lucas decided to rename *Revenge Of The Jedi* as *Return Of The Jedi* because revenge was not a Jedi attitude. Positive emotions are what saves the galaxy and the Skywalker legacy. "Mom, you say the biggest problem in this universe is nobody helps each other,"Anakin says, stating Lucas' theme of the need for compassion in the world, between individuals and on a wider scale. For all their war story connotations, the *Star Wars* films are very much a rallying cry for harmony at a personal and communal level. "He gives without any sense of reward," Shmi says to Qui-Gon, verbalising Lucas' concentration on compassion in the episodes that will follow.

In *The Phantom Menace*, the concept of freedom at both an individual and communal level is expressed through the slavery of Anakin and his mother. After winning his freedom from slavery Anakin promises to return and free the slaves.

As in *A New Hope*, the repetition of a dinner scene gives the characters and settings a root in a familiar earthly routine. It also crystallizes and encapsulates the core theme of the film whilst amplifying the believability of these fantasy characters.

The skill of Lucas and his design team at condensing and symbolising a dramatic purpose is evident in the colour schemes and shapes. Maul's ship is like a knife cutting through space. The curvilinear sweep of the bright yellow Naboo fighters is delicate and also looks too pretty to really go up against the ugly, angular might of the bad guys.

Clearly, Lucas enjoys using this story to establish the concept of The Force through Qui-Gon Jinn's relationship with Anakin. Qui-Gon is the only one with real faith in Anakin's ability. Padmé's face only registers doubt. Qui-Gon is always instructing: "Remember, concentrate on the moment. Feel, don't think. Use your instincts." This encouragement is a precursor to the guidance Luke will receive from Yoda.

In keeping with the sense of destiny that pervades the entire saga, Qui-Gon comments to Shmi that his meeting with Anakin "…was not a coincidence. Nothing happens by accident." This line gives another perspective on all that unfolds in the huge story that follows.

The issue of change and going with the flow takes us back to *THX 1138* and *American Graffiti*. "I don't want things to change," says Anakin. "You can't stop the change, anymore than you can stop the suns from setting," Shmi replies.

The film plays to Lucas' sense of cinema by creating emotion through motion. The pod-racing sequence is a little overlong, and arguably one of the weaker moments in the entire span of the saga. Nonetheless, it demonstrates Lucas' skills in the use of editing, sound and the integration of live action, miniatures and computer-generated environments to create a moment. You really feel as though you are in the pod. Lucas refines the feeling he has been after ever since *A New Hope* with Luke in the X-Wing. Every *Star Wars* movie has such a sequence and no doubt a race and chase will figure in *Episode III*. The weakness of the pod race scene is not because of its duration but because there is no character moment for Anakin. In the Gungan sub sequence, each character's essential traits are displayed as the little ship drifts through the sea. In the pod race, there is nothing as defined as this. Sure, Anakin wins the race through cunning and determination but it might perhaps have been even more involving for him to have him more obviously use The Force latent in him, though at this time he is unaware of his Force potential. Lucas lets the action speak for itself. Anakin wins because of determination, especially since he was the last to leave the starting grid and had never even completed a race before.

The environments symbolise the drama. For example, the Jedi Council is lit by natural light and the sense of unity and connection is made very real by the pattern on the floor, a circle with a motif of flourishing wings or flames, fanning out and signifying energy. Contrast this with Senator Palpatine's blood-red décor. The Jedi Council is an unfussy, minimalist space, light and airy. The Naboo palace fuses a slightly Medieval and Renaissance look with the hi-tech in Lucas' most obvious visual nod to *Flash Gordon*. Williams' music over the Naboo rescue scenes evokes the swashbuckling tempo of Erich Wolfgang Korngold's music for *The Adventures Of Robin Hood* (1938).

Lucas continues the motif of appearances being deceptive. Who would think that the clumsy and goofy Jar-Jar Binks would be so pivotal in the Gungan victory precisely because of his so-called flaws. It is the *Dumbo* ethos: what held you down will take you up and up and up. Like Dumbo, Jar-Jar even has big ears.

The film is a busy refinement of Lucas' approach reaching right back to *THX 1138*. We are immersed in this other world, with even more fervour than usual, and it is so detailed and filled with incidental action, just like real life, that we really find it a credible place. Just witness the sequence when Qui-Gon and company enter Mos Espa on Tatooine as they pass through the crowds. The detail of activity makes this world concrete. Lucas continues to echo the other movies. Qui-Gon's poncho recalls and anticipates that worn by Luke Skywalker. *Star Wars* is like outer space by Charles Dickens. It is warm, comic, inventive, dense. Lucas roots the unfamiliar in one of the most familiar ritual of all, a family sharing a meal. Immediately, we are no longer in space. We are in our own homes, in our own world.

How would Lucas top Darth Vader's visage? By opposing it. Where Vader was masked and armoured, Darth Maul is simply tattooed and robed. Maul is elementally evil, his horned head readily suggesting images of the Devil familiar to so many.

Background: After 1983, Lucas worked on everything except *Star Wars*, stating that someday he would get back to it. Lucas' return to the *Star Wars* story after sixteen years was heralded with great anticipation and suggested that he is the Charles Dickens of the stars. Just what would the story be about? And in turn just what ideas and issues would work their way into the narrative? A long time prior to *The Phantom Menace*, Lucas made it clear that the first three episodes would chart Anakin Skywalker's path to the Dark Side of The Force to become Darth Vader. Lucas has often likened the *Star Wars* story to a symphony with repeating motifs and forms. This is also very evident in the visual design of the film, notably in the characters' costumes and appearance. A look says as much as a line of dialogue in Lucas' very visual world.

In November 1994, Lucas commenced writing the screenplay for what would become *The Phantom Menace*. Truly independent of studio approval at this stage, Lucas developed the script in tangent with a small art design team at Skywalker Ranch. Lucas had initially approached Frank Darabont (writer/director of *The Shawshank Redemption* (1995), *The Green Mile* (1999) and *The Majestic* (2001)) to write the screenplay. Darabont had written work for Lucas before on *The Young Indiana Jones Chronicles* in the early 1990s. As Lucas developed the screenplay, the designs for characters, locales, vehicles etc. took shape under the guidance of Doug Chiang. Illustrator Ian McCaig was brought in to develop certain characters, notably Darth Maul. Inevitably huge amounts of material never made the filming stage, including air whales which were to have been ridden by Gungans in the end battle above the fields. The air whales were inspired by Ralph McQuarrie designs of the late 1970s for *The Empire Strikes Back* where they were to have featured in the skies of Bespin.

The film was shot at Leavesden Studios outside London, Whippendell Woods, Heaver Castle and Tunisia. Lucas utilised the digital backlot idea in order to reduce production costs. Backgrounds were built inside the computer.

Verdict: Expansive and glorious, if sometimes lacking in enough recognisable human behaviour, *The Phantom Menace* contains a rich seam of emotions contrasting with the simpler high spirits of *A New Hope*. 3/5

Star Wars: Episode II: Attack Of The Clones (2002)

Cast: Hayden Christensen (Anakin Skywalker), Ewan McGregor (Obi-Wan Kenobi), Natalie Portman (Padmé Amidala), Samuel L Jackson (Mace Windu), Frank Oz (Yoda), Anthony Daniels (C-3PO), Kenny Baker (R2D2), Ian McDiarmid (Senator Palpatine), Christopher Lee (Count Dooku), Daniel Logan (Boba Fett), Leanna Walsman (Zam Wesell), Temeura Morrison (Jango Fett), Ahmed Best (Jar-Jar Binks), Pernilla August (Shmi Skywalker), Jimmy Smits (Bail Organa), Ayesha Darker (Queen Jamilla), Olivier Ford Davies (Sio Bibble), Ronald Falk (Dexter Jettster), Joel Edgerton (Owen Lars), Bonnie Piesse (Beru Whitesun), Jack Thomson (Cliegg Lars).

Crew: Director/Story: George Lucas; Screenplay: George Lucas & Jonathan Hales; Producer: Rick McCallum; Director of Photography: David Tattersall; Production Design: Gavin Bouquet; Concept Design Supervisors: Doug Chiang, Erik Tiemens, Ryan Church; Costume Designer: Trisha Biggar; Editor: Ben Burtt; Music: John Williams; Special Visual Effects: Industrial Light and Magic. Twentieth Century-Fox. 142 mins.

Story: Set ten years after the events of *The Phantom Menace*, this second instalment follows Anakin Skywalker as a young man, falling in love with Padmé Amidala and wrestling to reconcile his personal and Jedi commitments. The story continues to explore the dangerous influence of the Trade Federation Chancellor Palpatine and Darth Sidious that was left hanging menacingly at the end of the previous episode. Obi-Wan Kenobi and Anakin are charged with protecting Padmé and Anakin is keen to uncover the intrigue surrounding her. Anakin and Obi-Wan alternately spar and banter like father and son. On Coruscant, Padmé is attacked by a bounty hunter named Zam Wesell who uses a Kyber dart as her weapon. Anakin escorts Padmé back to the assumed safety of Naboo where he meets her family. Obi-Wan's investigations lead him to the one planet where the Kyber dart poison is made, a water world named Kamino. On Kamino, Obi-Wan discovers a clone army manufacturing facility, its source cells coming from the bounty hunter Jango Fett. Jango is given a clone son, Boba. On Naboo, Anakin dreams of his mother and is sure she is in danger. Anakin confesses his love for

Padmé who swiftly falls in love with him. Together they travel to Tatooine where they hook up with the Lars family, including Owen and Beru. Shmi is married to Cliegg Lars but she is nowhere to be seen. She has been taken captive by Tusken Raiders. Anakin goes looking for her, finding her near death at a Tusken Raider camp. Anakin slays the Tusken Raiders in revenge and returns to the Lars homestead where Shmi is buried. On Kamino, Obi-Wan learns that Jango Fett killed the bounty hunter who tried to assassinate Padmé and Obi-Wan races off to confront Fett on the rock planet of Geonosis. Obi-Wan is taken prisoner by Dooku and the waspy Geonosians. Anakin and Padmé arrive to rescue Obi-Wan and are themselves imprisoned alongside him in a gladiatorial arena. Confronted by huge beasts, our heroes liberate themselves and are then aided by the arrival of several hundred Jedi, led by Mace Windu and Yoda. Travelling with them are the Clone army. An immense air and ground battle ensues in which countless Jedi die. Anakin and Obi-Wan go to confront Dooku, who is in league with Darth Sidious, and a duel ensues. Obi-Wan and Anakin are injured and Yoda comes to their aid before confronting Dooku himself, summoning all his Jedi force. Dooku escapes. Anakin and Padmé marry on Naboo.

Themes And Subtext: Compassion and selflessness versus passion and the abuse of power. Anakin talks to Padmé about compassion on their way to Naboo at the beginning of the film. Sidious and Dooku represent greed and The Dark Side symbolises selfishness and fear. Obi-Wan Kenobi talked of The Clone Wars in *A New Hope*. Now Lucas shows us what sparked the Clone Wars. In the *Star Wars* universe the power of the individual is placed within the surge of communal effort. This individualism walks a fine line between victory and failure. It is as much celebrated as questioned. Clones represent the most obvious disregard for individualism and all the frailties that entails. The film takes the muted feeling at Qui-Gon's funeral in *The Phantom Menace* and amplifies it.

Background: No sooner had *The Phantom Menace* been released than work began on what became titled *Attack Of The Clones*. Lucas again synchronised his work on the script with an Art Department team developing character designs, sometimes using designs that had not been incorporated into *The Phantom Menace*. Lucas collaborated on the screenplay with Jonathan Hales, who had written seven episodes of *The Young Indiana Jones Chronicles*, and it was completed just days before production began in June 2000.

Attack Of The Clones was shot in Sydney, Australia, at the Twentieth Century-Fox studios with additional shooting in March 2001 and very early November 2001 at Ealing and Elstree Studios in London.

Lucas' career-long ambition to develop applications of digital technology resulted in this film being shot on high definition (HD) digital video, using a camera developed by Sony and Panavision. No film was used. In 1981 a feature film called *Julia Julia* was shot on high definition video and transferred to film. *Attack of the Clones* was shot on a Sony HDW-F900 camcorder using Panavision Primo Digital Lenses. For Lucas it meant that material shot could be immediately reviewed without waiting for the rushes to come back the next day. From a production standpoint using video is more budget- and schedule-friendly than film. One key issue with the use of the new HD camera was the kind of lenses that would be available to create the necessary widescreen effect. On the set of *Attack Of The Clones*, an area was set up for Lucas and Tattersall to monitor the material and fine-tune it. On the set itself, Lucas monitored the scene being shot on large 42-inch flat screen plasma monitors. Unlike a film camera, which takes five minutes to reload and prepare a fresh spool, the video camera only needed to be reloaded once a day. Rick McCallum, in an interview with *American Cinematographer* in the October 2001 issue, explained that another advantage of video is that at the end of each day videotaped material was assembled in the edit suite for immediate review. Once footage had been shot it would be transmitted to California where ILM would work on it and then email it back to the location, making use of the time zone difference.

Aesthetically, debates continue about even the best quality video still not being as subtle as film. The September 2001 issue of *American Cinematographer* included an interview with Lucas and Rick McCallum about these issues and their ways of working. Lucas commented, "I'm interested in the emotional impact of the lighting and the framing and how that moves in time. That's what I care about." Lucas went on to explain that there are computer programs to make digital video look like different types of film stock. The film features around 2,200 effects shots, all digitally created and making it logical to shoot live action digitally rather than go to the expense of converting from one format to another. The film's visual effects are dreamlike at points and really do look like production illustrations brought to life. Just as *The Empire Strikes Back* extended the technique and framing of Ray Harryhausen's stop motion effects, in *Attack Of The Clones* his legacy is revised in the Geonosis arena battle. The animation of Yoda is notable for the subtlety of facial expression. The fabric of the Kaminoans clothes moves believably. The film is less sure with some of its comedy, notably when it involves C-3PO. Where *The Phantom Menace* had a bright look, the sequel emphasises light and shadow. *The Phantom Menace* was bright just as young Anakin's future was bright. In this film, Anakin's path is less certain. By the end of *Attack Of The Clones*, the skies are blood red.

Lucas often uses the serial like a symphony by repeating and reconfiguring images and moments from one episode in other episodes. For this episode, we see reinterpretations of Luke and Leia's chasm scene in *A New Hope* and the Rancor scene from *Return Of The Jedi*.

Lucas' cinéma-vérité approach remains and adds immediacy to the Geonosis war sequence with its quick zooms on soldiers in aircraft. Lucas often uses the zoom lens, notably in a shot of Anakin learning of the fate of his mother.

Themes And Subtext: With *Attack Of The Clones*, Lucas amplifies the drama of the first instalment and stays true to his promise that each chapter carries cumulative power and throws into relief what has gone before. The film riffs on the comforts and anxieties in the repetitions of family history.

The Tatooine sequence is a mini-Western with melancholy and austere, wide compositions emphasising the barren landscape that matches the feelings at work. In *A New Hope*, film savvy critics noted that the image of the burning Lars homestead recalled *The Searchers*. *Attack Of The Clones* repeats the reference with the Shmi Skywalker storyline. The future home of Luke Skywalker is a desert wilderness, and the Skywalker family have their adventures in the wilderness of space. These are powerful variations and continuations of American narrative figureheads such as Natty Bumppo (in James Fenimore Cooper's *Leather-*

stocking tales), Huckleberry Finn and Dorothy Gale as they journey through a world of clashing cultures, oppressed people, lifestyles destroyed, new worlds and possibilities discovered.

Lucas' beloved motif of the student and mentor gets full play, with both positive and negative consequences. The potential of young people, the heart of the story, gets a clear statement when Yoda and the young Jedi students help Obi-Wan locate Kamino. Yoda says, "Truly wonderful the mind of a child is."

Lucas elicits strong performances from all his cast, drawing on the power of a glance or an intonation to convey more than the words themselves. There is a warmth to Anakin and Obi-Wan's relationship, notably at the start of the film when Obi-Wan assures Anakin that Padmé was pleased to see him. Obi-Wan is a much more forceful presence than in *The Phantom Menace*. In this film he is urgent (especially when he berates Anakin for wanting to jump from the gunship to help Padmé during the battle), funny and understanding. Anakin is sullen, surly and melancholic. As Anakin enters the arena watch for his brief and regretful glance at Obi-Wan. When Lucas was casting the part he hinted at wanting a James Dean quality to the Anakin performance. Anakin and Obi-Wan's bickering recalls the father/son relationship of Henry Jones Senior and Indiana Jones in *Indiana Jones And The Last Crusade*. Padmé Amidala kicks into real Princess Leia mode in the moment when she and Anakin depart Tatooine and Natalie Portman's performance is at its best in the Naboo scenes.

The film works well because it foregrounds recognisable emotions so clearly and directly. The love story arc is told with brevity in keeping with Lucas' description of this part of the story as "a love haiku more than a love sonnet." (*Vanity Fair*, March 2002) Whereas the camerawork is frequently stationary or uses a long lens through much of the film, for the picnic scene the camera tracks gracefully and perfectly around Anakin and Padmé, emphasising the grace and idyll of the moment. For their first kiss the shallow focus obliterates the world around them. The moment is all that matters. When they marry at the end of the story, they look to a cloudy horizon in a shot that mirrors the final image of Luke, Leia and the droids in *The Empire Strikes Back*. Amidst the chaos and sweep of the action, some of the strongest moments of the films are the smallest such as Anakin touching Padmé's naked shoulder blade or Padmé looking with concern at Anakin when he first levitates an object. John Williams' love theme for the film evokes his theme for the 1972 television movie *Jane Eyre*.

With Lucas' use of cloning as a central plot issue and motif he returns to the concerns of *THX 1138*, where society is endangered when it becomes unthinking and unfeeling, though the clone soldiers display some independent thought during the battle. The *Star Wars* story celebrates the independent, thinking, feeling, spontaneous spirit that is connected to the larger need.

Verdict: All its life, *Star Wars* has been acknowledged as a B-movie. With *Attack Of The Clones*, Lucas has crafted the most B-movie *Star Wars* film yet and one of the strongest. The film boldly intercuts between lavish, detailed and believable environments, yet finds a very human level to the drama that rarely gets lost amidst the scale of the emerging war. One criticism levelled at the first episode was that it was not warm enough. This film rectifies the charge. Lucas has never been a director prone to drawing huge displays of emotion from his characters but in this film he anchors the spectacle and weaves in and out of it anger, regret and fear. A melancholic and gargantuan film. 4/5

Throughout the *Star Wars* story, both on screen and in its production, the influence of mythology has been acknowledged. These reference points and inspirations have given the *Star Wars* narrative a pop culture standing shared by only a few stories.

Star Wars is a completely American tale, as much a version of that country's relatively recent mythology as it is of more ancient tales. America has used the potent image of the frontier to create a self-image and *Star Wars* is part of that tradition. Lucas has talked about his metaphoric use of space as a frontier - in *Star Wars* the frontier is external and geographical, internal and emotional. The power and pull of these films emphasise a continuing place for stories that lay out common conflicts and hopes in vividly broad strokes. In his landmark study of American literature, *Regeneration Through Violence: The Mythology Of The American Frontier*, Richard Slotkin writes: 'American hero figures and metaphors for the American experience were not so much derived from... nature as they were from extended experience in the wilderness.'

Beyond the galaxies, the monsters, the duels, the near misses and close calls, the *Star Wars* story for all its sound and fury is concerned simply with peace; the peace of the individual heart and mind, and the heart and mind of a world. Our world.

4: Team Coach - Films As Producer

"I don't consider anything ever really finished."

George Lucas,
George Lucas: The Creative Impulse, p.160

Continuing Adventures

After the intense experience of directing *A New Hope*, Lucas focused on writing, producing and broadening the activities of his company, seeing himself more as coach than player.

One of the first things he did was *The Star Wars Holiday Special*, a CBS TV show broadcast in December 1978. The special centres on Chewbacca's family, his wife Mala, father Itchy and son Lumpy. Chewie's mission is to get to his home and family to celebrate Life Day. Carrie Fisher, Mark Hamill and Harrison Ford all appear as their *Star Wars* characters and the show features musical numbers and an animated segment.

Lucas' first feature after *A New Hope* was a sequel to *American Graffiti*. Far less buoyant than the original, partly because of its setting in time, the film did not meet with the warmth and popularity of its predecessor. *More American Graffiti* was executive-produced by Lucas with a screenplay by its director BWL Norton. The film follows the same multi-narrative format as the original, though without the unity of location. Howard Kazanjian, Lucas' old film school friend, produced the movie. The film is set around several successive New Year's Eves in the 1960s. Steve and Laurie are preparing for their fourth child, John Milner is still racing cars and Terry is in Vietnam. Debbie lives with a guitar player and even Bob Falfa grows up - as a cop. The vignettes include a peace demonstration. The film demonstrates Lucas' love of revisiting characters in the various worlds he has created - documenting their pasts, presents and futures.

With *More American Graffiti* completed and with *American Graffiti* in re-release on the back of *Star Wars*' success, Lucas focused on continuing the Skywalker adventure. Happy to not direct the next instalment, Lucas devised the story and selected an older director, Irvin Kershner, who had taught Lucas at USC, to helm the movie. Production began in 1979 in Finse, Norway. The production then moved to Elstree Studios for the remainder of the shoot. Lucas spent most of his time in San Rafael overseeing the visual effects. Although Lucas did not direct the sequels they are perceived as George Lucas films rather in the way that one does not really think of *Gone With The Wind* (referenced in one of the posters for *The Empire Strikes Back*) as a Victor Fleming film but rather a film of its producer, David O Selznick.

The Empire Strikes Back was released in May 1980 and was a huge hit. Its fidelity to the original and expansion of its breath are a testament to Lucas' producing skills.

The Empire Strikes Back stood in strong contrast to its predecessor. Where *A New Hope* was bright and breezy, *Empire* was brooding. Lucas initially brought in Leigh Brackett who had written hard-boiled and western scripts since the 1940s, notably for Howard Hawks, suggesting Lucas was looking for that kind of tough-talking, human dialogue which emphasised the group dynamic of characters. Brackett died leaving Lucas without a writer to continue drafting. At about the same time, new writer Lawrence Kasdan who had just had a script produced by Spielberg (*Continental Divide*) and had just written *Raiders Of The Lost Ark* (in 1978) was then asked by Lucas if he would like to develop the screenplay for *The Empire Strikes Back*. Kasdan accepted, writing a screenplay which fused the rules of the game with rich characterisation. Structurally, the film confidently intercuts between Luke's time with Yoda and Han and Leia's adventures for the mid portion of the film. It is a luxurious-looking film, in contrast to *A New Hope*. Director Irvin Kershner invested the characters' performances with nuance and maturity. Check the comic scene with Luke, Leia and Han as Luke lies on his hospital bed. The scene plays up the teenage spirit of Lucas' good-guy galaxy. Kershner and his crew continue the *cinéma-vérité* approach of the first film: the zoom-out from Han and Luke on Hoth makes the audience feel like a helpless observer; the 'helicopter' shot that takes us towards the tauntaun galloping across the snow. The visuals are elegant. Kershner amplifies Vader's absence of humanity by repeatedly using his black mass in silhouette. Characters doubt themselves and face failure. "I'm not afraid," Luke says to his teacher, Yoda, to which Yoda menacingly replies, "You will be, You will be." The film is Luke's apocalypse now as everything he trusted in and cared about falls away.

With the death of John Barry as production designer, (he had most famously worked on *2001: A Space Odyssey*, the original *Star Wars* and *Superman: The Movie*), Norman Reynolds was hired. Reynolds went on to *Raiders Of The Lost Ark*, *Young Sherlock Holmes*, *Return To Oz* and many other films. Dennis Muren supervised visual effects at Industrial Light and Magic, with Phil Tippett responsible for the stop-motion animation work with his colleague Jon Berg. Paul Hirsch edited the picture, always keeping the intercutting narrative clear.

The film allowed Lucas to embellish images and ideas from *A New Hope*, notably the definition and function of The Force. The white world of Cloud City is evocative of *THX 1138*. The sequences around the carbon freezing chamber are perhaps the best and for a really insightful read into the creation of this part of the film and the film as a whole read *Once Upon A Galaxy*.

The brutal and cruel lightsabre duel at the climax results in Luke hanging from Cloud City calling for help, seemingly abandoned. The pain, uncertainty, doubt and deception in this film are emblematic of real fairy tales which always have their dark sides.

At the same time as the new *Star Wars* film, Lucas executive-produced with Francis Ford Coppola on *Kagemusha*, directed by Akira Kurosawa. Kurosawa's samurai films (*Seven Samurai*, *Yojimbo*, *Hidden Fortress*) were important to Lucas. The *Star Wars* double trilogy is heavily informed by Japanese culture and Kurosawa's historical films in its design, framing and composition. *Kagemusha* (meaning Shadow Warrior) tells of a warlord who uses a decoy so that he can focus on his clan's ascendancy to power over Japan. When the warlord is killed his double must really take control and maintain troop morale. It is an epic and glorious historical drama.

Fedoras First, Lightsabres Last

In 1980, after the success of *The Empire Strikes Back*, Lucas began building the Skywalker Ranch in Marin County, northern California, which today serves as Lucas' administrative base as well as being home to an art department and post-production facilities. Work is currently under way on a new building at Big Rock Ranch, adjoining Skywalker Ranch, designed in the manner of Frank Lloyd Wright's prairie style of stone and brick. The Ranch is also home to the Lucasfilm Archives, a library and has its own fire service and softball pitch.

In the early 1970s, Lucas conceived of a boyish adventuring archaeologist. Presenting the idea to Spielberg in 1977, the project was eventually filmed in 1980 and released in 1981 as *Raiders Of The Lost Ark*. The film extended Lucas' run of hits. Lucas conceived the Indiana Jones character and the world in which he adventured. Spielberg and Kasdan embellished the material and Lucas engineered a very lithe production which Spielberg brought in ahead of schedule, perhaps slightly in reaction to the overlong shoot of his previous feature, *1941*. *Raiders Of The Lost Ark* was a story told even faster than the *Star Wars* films. For many cinema-goers it was a completely fresh experience despite having its roots so clearly in adventure serials from the 1950s. Children in 1981 would have been completely unaware of the film's sources. The film was very positively received and helped boost Harrison Ford's career as a huge movie star. Lucas once said that if he could be a dream figure he would be Indy. The character combines both physical and intellectual competence as well as being very charismatic. Lucas explained early on in developing the script that Jones was a role model for children. Jones generates meaning in his life by moving beyond the regular world, assuming a new identity in contrast with his mild professorial manner as seen at the opening and close of the film. His adventure sees him facing the presumed death of his partner and kicks off with him being double-crossed. These are very simple presentations of dilemma but for a young audience particularly they hit home and make quite an impression. Jones is tested by his adventure and emerges victorious with the help of his friends and some supernatural intervention. Does that sound familiar? *Raiders Of The Lost Ark* opened Hollywood's eyes to the action film format which then really kicked into high gear a few years later with *Die Hard*. *Raiders* is infused with charm and has a romantic sensibility about the world and the movie heritage it invokes.

In contrast Lucas gave his support and advice to Lawrence Kasdan on his directorial debut, *Body Heat* (1981). Lucas asked not to receive an on-screen credit for the film, which was one of the best adult dramas to come out of Hollywood in the 1980s, with its fusion of film noir, femmes fatales and a 1980s slickness.

In 1982, Lucas returned to his early love, animation. He executive-produced a quirky feature directed by his old pal John Korty in collaboration with Charles Swenson. *Twice Upon A Time* was an inventive animated feature which used a process dubbed lumage (luminous image) in which the cut-out characters were illuminated from below. For all its freshness, the film did not generate much interest. It was certainly not akin to the classical style of animation that most people are familiar with from Disney features. The film was the first production between Lucasfilm and The Ladd Company and was scored by former Doobie Brother, Michael McDonald. At the time of its release it was the only animated feature in general release other than Don Bluth's *The Secret Of NIMH;* a reminder of how far animation has come in almost twenty years. In an interview with *Starlog* magazine (issue 66) Korty said of *Twice Upon A Time*: "I wanted to make a movie that would be funny and entertaining and contained animated characters. But I also wanted it to include the message that reality is not so bad after all and that what you need to stay sane in this world is some combination of fantasy and reality." Sadly, the film never really connected with audiences despite its freshness and invention. It was not the first time that Lucas would support a fairy tale-inspired story - he went on to support *Labyrinth* (1986) and *The Land Before Time*.

In 1983 *Return Of The Jedi* was released to draw a close to the *Star Wars* saga at that time. It was directed by Richard Marquand from a screenplay by Lawrence Kasdan and George Lucas, based on Lucas' story. As well as resolving the plot, it clarified Lucas' thematic concerns. Film critic and screenwriter Jay Cocks (*Strange Days*, *The Age Of Innocence*) wrote that with each episode of the serial the narrative stakes got higher and higher.

Jedi is the most expansive of the trilogy. Its final movement focuses on Luke and Darth Vader and is affecting in its conflict between anger, raging emotion, peace and stillness. The film is very similar to *The Phantom Menace* in its structure and like that film pits a nature-based culture (the Ewoks) against the supposed technological and military might of a huge, technological mindset and its army. The Ewoks were a development of Lucas' original (and forever intriguing) concept of having Wookies trained by the Rebellion to fly ships against the Empire. When Lucas had established Chewie's piloting dexterity he had to reconfigure the image of a technologically unsophisticated culture. The filming of the Ewok scenes was done in Crescent City in Northern California. Yuma in Arizona became Tatooine for the terrific Sail Barge rescue sequence and Elstree studios was home to scenes for the Ewok village, Jabba's palace, Rebel and Imperial ship interiors, the Death Star and the Emperor's Throne Room (originally conceived as a lair in a cave, engulfed by lava). The now-named Crescent City had once been home to the Miwok native American tribe which may be the source of inspiration for the Ewok name. Other say that Ewok is just wookie spelt sideways.

Jedi is at its most emotional in the scene between Leia and Luke in the Ewok village, and later when Luke and Vader battle under the evil watch of The Emperor who implores Luke to strike down his father. When Luke finally unleashes his anger there is a real sense of release. Enhancing the believability of the scene are several hand-held shots of their duel which bring you into the conflict. John Williams' score reverberates with a doom-laden choir which connects the end of the story with the first episode where a more flamboyant and melodramatic chorus accompanies the three-way duel at the end of that film.

The invention and fanciful design of this final episode testifies to Lucas' resources and also his independence. Lucas and his team were able to make the film exactly as they wanted to. Industrial Light & Magic, who quipped that the film was their doctoral thesis, was once more led by Dennis Muren with Phil Tippett overseeing creature creation, notably the Rancor. The monster was originally to have been a performer in a suit but ultimately the team achieved the effect with a rod puppet within a miniature cave setting. The realisation of the Rancor is not only believable on account of its motion and scale but also the application of editing and lighting. In both *Return Of The Jedi* and *The Phantom Menace* the big guns lose as Ewoks and Gungans fight with passion to protect their homes against invasion. Lucas' emphasis on peace and non-aggression receives its clearest statement as Luke refuses to fight his father.

The entire saga (at the time just three episodes) is wrapped up in this final episode. When Lucas completes the first three episodes the sense of culmination should be impressive and the prequel story will inevitably create new textures and ironies as well as lend power to the second trilogy. Like *The Phantom Menace*, this last chapter has a three-way ending: in space, on land and in a temple-like arena. Lucas' editing patterns propel the story along at quite a speed. *Jedi*'s highpoint for action on land is the Sail Barge sequence, a truly swashbuckling sequence and one of the *Star Wars* cycle's best. After all its chaos and noise, *Jedi* ends on a powerfully small and near silent note with Luke at the funeral pyre of his father (shot at Skywalker Ranch) followed by an Ewok celebration. The very last shot is a simple one of our heroes huddled together as though for a family snapshot. For all the spectacle and fury, the final image is of people, united and happy.

With *Jedi* completed, Lucas felt he had spent enough time in the stars (almost ten years) and he announced something of a sabbatical. It was not that much of an absence.

From The Temple Of Doom To Saturday Morning Cartoons

In 1984, Lucasfilm released *Indiana Jones And The Temple Of Doom*. The film was quite different to *Raiders Of The Lost Ark* and was told at a faster pace, with more comedy and a darker tone. The film received criticism for its intensity. Lucas' game plan was to contrast the bright and breezy *Raiders Of The Lost Ark* with a darker, more intense story second time around, rather like he did with *The Empire Strikes Back*. In very simple strokes, Lucas' story presents a story of good and evil with Indiana Jones' sense of justice marking the turning point of the story. The retrieval of the Sankara Stones is no longer the most important thing - the retrieval of the enslaved children is. As with all the *Star Wars* movies and also *Raiders Of The Lost Ark*, *Indiana Jones And The Temple Of Doom* has its speed-kick moment in the form of the minecart chase which brilliantly integrates live action, practical effects work with blue screen and also miniature photography. The sequence is a terrific example of pre-digital visual effects design and execution enhanced by vivid sound design. The film has a warmer ending than *Raiders Of The Lost Ark*.

Although he had left the *Star Wars* movie universe behind in 1983, Lucas made a return to one quiet corner of it in 1984 with *The Ewok Adventure*, a family TV-movie aired in November 1984. It began as a one-hour story but as work progressed the narrative expanded. The film was shot in northern California and told of a family whose starcruiser crashes on Endor. The story focuses on the two children Mace and Cindel Towani as they spend time with the Ewoks, including Wicket, the Ewok who befriends Princess Leia in *Return Of The Jedi*, and must rescue their parents from the Gorax. *The Ewok Adventure* was directed by John Korty from a script by Bob Carrau based on a Lucas story. It was released theatrically in Europe as *Caravan Of Courage: The Ewok Adventure* in Christmas 1984. The project proved successful enough for a follow-up, *The Battle For Endor* in which Cindel Towani is the human focus. She befriends a hermit named Noa (Wilfred Brimley) and his pet Ewok Teek, who moves at lighting speed through the trees. Together they help the Ewoks fight off Terak the Marauder and his stooges. Other Ewoks are imprisoned by an evil witch, Charal, and must be rescued from the castle. This follow-up Ewok adventure was more action-orientated than its predecessor. In a way, Lucas' fidelity to the fairy-tale format is admirable in its single-mindedness. One of the key creative personnel on the project was *Star Wars* ace, Joe Johnston who went on to direct.

At one point, Lucas was approached to run the Disney studio but declined. However, he developed with them the *Star Tours* theme park attraction which opened in spring 1987.

In a further expansion of the *Star Wars* universe, Lucas executive-produced two *Star Wars* animated series, *Ewoks* and *Droids: The Adventures Of R2-D2 And C-3PO*. They premiered on Saturday, 7 September 1985 and were screened back-to-back forming an hour of programming. *Droids* centred on the various new masters that C-3PO and R2-D2 served under. *Ewoks* explored all of Endor for its stories. Where *Droids* arranged its stories into blocks of four episodes telling one story arc, each *Ewoks* episode was self-contained. The series were produced by Nelvana Animation who had created the animation for the *Star Wars Holiday Special* that aired on American TV in 1978 and which gave the world its first look at Boba Fett, albeit in animated form. Ben Burtt wrote the Mungo Baobab stories for *Droids* and Joe Johnston wrote 'Coby And The Starhunters.' One of today's top animation writers, Paul Dini, started out writing on *Ewoks*. Most animated shows at that time comprised of 8-10,000 cels of animation, but some *Droids* episodes had up to 24,000 cels, and so the quality of movement and expression was infinitely superior. *Droids* lasted one season and *Ewoks* lasted two, symptomatic of *Star Wars'* waning mainstream popularity in the mid to late 1980s, before its return in 1991.

In 1984/85, Lucas' old friend Walter Murch made his only film as a director, the sombre *Return To Oz*. When Murch needed a little help and advice during the shoot, Lucas flew from Japan to be at his pal's side. Spielberg and Coppola also lent a hand.

Lucas' other major effort in 1985 was his reteaming with Coppola to back the funding and production of Paul Schrader's brilliant film *Mishima*, an examination of various aspects of the life of Japanese writer Yukio Mishima. It was a Zoetrope, Filmlink, Lucasfilm co-production. Mishima was a writer who wanted to remind Japan of its heritage as he watched his homeland change after the Western world's capitalist ethos. The film is stunning, particularly in its dramatisations of moments in Mishima's novels. Lucas' love of Eastern culture and the fusion of it with Western narratives now seem ahead of its time given the current interest in Tawainese, Chinese and Japanese cinema.

A Maze, An Intergalactic Duck, 3-D Dancing In Space

Keen to broaden his collaborations ever further, Lucas hooked up with the late, great Muppet ace Jim Henson on the film *Labyrinth* (1986). The film was a soft-centred, dreamy fantasy story populated by animatronic characters and two human performers, Jennifer Connelly and David Bowie. A very gentle film, it was not as big a hit as might have been hoped but it has stood the test of time well with its clear and simple themes about growing up well integrated into the fantastic environment. It is clear to see why the story must have appealed as it follows a teenage girl from this world venturing through the fantasy environment of a labyrinth to retrieve her baby brother who has been stolen by the goblins. The project had been on Jim Henson's mind for many years and was his follow-up to *The Dark Crystal* (co-produced by Gary Kurtz). There had been Lucas/Henson ties since the late 1970s and the development of Yoda for *The Empire Strikes Back*. In a way, Lucas has more in common with Henson than someone like Steven Spielberg. Henson's commitment to education through his work for young minds (on *Sesame Street*, for example) is certainly evident in Lucas' work today. Lucas came on board *Labyrinth* as an executive producer, working particularly on the development of the script and then in the editing process. Maybe Henson's sensibility stayed with Lucas. Jar-Jar Binks' effectiveness in *The Phantom Menace* testifies to this. Like *Star Wars*, the film is about a young person getting to grips with the world with help of unexpected allies. Like Dorothy in *The Wizard Of Oz*, Sarah in *Labyrinth* is returned safely home, her understanding of herself broadened by her adventure. *Labyrinth* has generated quite a following, particularly it seems amongst people who first saw it as teenagers on its original release.

Lucas' other feature presentation in 1986 was *Howard The Duck* which has a very surreal premise - an intelligent duck from Duck World is mysteriously transported to Earth and hangs out with a girl from a punk rock band. Based on Steve Gerber's comic strip published by Marvel Comics in the 1970s, the film failed because it was so obvious that Howard was a short person in a suit. However, for the climax it does have an excellent stop-motion monster courtesy of Phil Tippett and ILM. It was one of the big fantasy comedy releases of the summer of 1986, following movies like *Ghostbusters* and *Gremlins*, but it died big time at the box office. Lucas' interest in part must have been in its story of an unassuming character being charged with a mission and also trying to get out of a place he does not belong in.

On 12 September 1986, Disneyland premiered the most expensive short film ever made. Fifteen minutes long and costing about $15 million the film was *Captain EO*, a 3-D musical space adventure directed by Francis Ford Coppola. The film starred Michael Jackson, at that time at the peak of his popularity. For Jackson, the film clearly represented an opportunity to build on the *Thriller* video with another fanciful short film, steeped in genre traditions and maximum resources. Captain Eo is a space adventurer whose little spaceship crashlands on a dark and toxic planet. Eo is charged with the responsibility of taking a gift to the evil and hidden Supreme Leader: the gift of song and dance. Eo is confronted by the Space Witch (Angelica Huston) and her Whip Warriors but Eo and his space race pals ultimately transform her and her world with music and performance, the power of creativity and the imagination. In the space of a short film, *Captain Eo* celebrates the power of teamwork and positivity. Eo sings two songs: 'We Are Here To Change The World' and 'Another Part Of Me.' With its speeding space chase, laser bolts and cast of characters, this is like a mini *Star Wars* musical. *Captain Eo* is one of the best, most unusual and certainly not widely known of projects Lucas has been involved with. To date, it has only been seen by people who have visited the theme parks. *Star Wars* design veteran Joe Johnston was heavily involved in the film, designing Eo's cute little ship, and Rick Baker worked on make-up. The cinematography was by Vittorio Storaro, production designing by John Napier (who went on to be visual consultant on Spielberg's *Hook*), music by James Horner and editing by Walter Murch. The film is a distinctly 1980s riff on an always appealing theme - the power of the imagination to transform and improve. The film was shot in two weeks in summer 1985 using two cameras for the 3-D process. In that same year, Lucas supported his friend Haskell Wexler's film *Latino*, a politically charged piece about Nicaragua and the American intervention there.

76

Flashing Swords, Superfine Cars
And Little Lost Dinosaurs

Lucas made no show at cinemas in 1987. He was, in part, busy developing an interest in educational media which today forms the basis of The George Lucas Educational Foundation. He executive-produced two feature films for release in 1988, both of them major Lucasfilm productions. The first to be released was *Willow*. The first Lucas screen story since *Indiana Jones And The Temple Of Doom*, it came out of Lucas' initial work on the *Star Wars* script in the early 1970s. Lucas had attempted to buy the rights to *The Lord Of The Rings* at one time. The story of *Willow* is certainly like Tolkien. It was Lucas' self-acknowledged attempt to show that fantasy movies could work for a mass audience. Like *Willow*, Peter Jackson's adaptation of Tolkien's serial was shot in New Zealand.

The story of *Willow* centres on an insecure farmer named Willow Ufgood who must end the reign of Queen Bavmorda. Doesn't her name sound a little like 'bad mother,' just as Darth Vader suggests 'dark father'? Like Luke Skywalker in *A New Hope*, Willow is initially very reluctant to get involved but eventually with the encouragement of his family he accepts the mission. The film is a trek movie, rather like *The Phantom Menace* and *A New Hope*. Willow befriends a down-on-his-luck warrior named Madmartigan, who occupies the kind of story position that Han does in *Star Wars*. Madmartigan agrees to help Willow get the baby Elora Danan to the kingdom of Tir Asleen and defeat the reign of Bavmorda. The film, directed by Ron Howard, is packed with situations and spectacle. Again, Lucas demonstrates his skill at conceiving genuinely threatening villains who are never jokers or fools. Lucas' villains are always absolutely committed to their task.

Lucas first thought about *Willow* as far back as his earliest days developing *Star Wars*. Lucas said that at one point the main characters of *Star Wars* might have been portrayed by short people. When Lucas met Warwick Davis, who played the Ewok Wicket in *Return Of The Jedi* and in the two Ewok movies, Lucas knew he had found his Willow.

The female lead, Sorsha (portrayed by Joanne Whalley), is a vintage Lucas heroine, a strongheaded young woman in the mould of Laurie

Henderson and Princess Leia. The world that Willow lives in and adventures through is as vividly drawn as that of the *Star Wars* universe. Lucas' affinity for medieval Japan shines through as much of the conceptual art makes clear. Initial designs for Madmartigan (portrayed in the film by Val Kilmer) are very Eastern influenced. His on-screen appearance is part European knight, part Samurai and part Native American. Madmartigan has something of Han Solo and John Milner about him in his cockiness, roguish ways and initial reluctance to help out and risk cracking his cool image. It is clearly a character type that Lucas enjoys placing in stories to show their changing value system. Lucas populates the world with Nelwyn (Willow's race) and Daikini (the Big People) and uses the opening of the film to present the familiar Lucas motif of going beyond the safety of home. For Willow, the Daikini crossroads represent the threshold over which a bigger, unknown and dangerous world awaits. Like THX, Willow is brave enough to make the journey beyond the world he knows.

By 1986 Lucas was ready to put *Willow* into motion, bringing on board director Ron Howard and screenwriter Bob Dolman. Together, they spent a year fashioning the specifics of the screenplay based on Lucas' template story. Pre-production began at the end of 1986 and then *Willow* was shot on location in Great Britain, New Zealand and at Elstree Studios. The film's climactic battle outside Bavmorda's castle was shot in a slate quarry in North Wales and is Lucas' clearest homage to Kurosawa's *The Seven Samurai* with its warriors fighting in the thrashing rain. Industrial Light and Magic handled the visual effects from their base in San Rafael, California. The narrative combined numerous references to fairy tales and legends. For example, the opening of the film recalls the story of Moses. As with the *Star Wars* films, Lucas places the characters in contrasting environments: the forest of the Nelwyn community living peaceably with themselves and the lush, green land; the snow-capped mountains that form the central phase of the journey; the stark and dark castle of Bavmorda. The film culminates with a celebration in the restored kingdom of Tir Asleen, the castle draped with banners. Sorsha and Madmartigan, having spent the adventure sparring and bickering, are together, cradling Elora. Lucas even find a way to bring in something of *A Midsummer Night's Dream* with the magic disyt that makes people fall in love.

Lucas brought the great French artist Jean 'Moebius' Giraud on board to provide production design concepts. Moebius' contributions suggest Lucas' push for a strongly Eastern design, combined with the more Northern European images of castles and rough hillsides. The book *Industrial Light And Magic: Into The Digital Era* (1996) includes several pieces of Moebius art for *Willow*, including a very fanciful and powerful imagining of General Kael. (Kael was portrayed by Pat Roach, who had previously fought Indiana Jones under the plane in *Raiders Of The Lost Ark* and thrown Indy into a mine cart in *Indiana Jones And The Temple Of Doom*.)

In visual effects history, *Willow* is a bridge between the old and the new technologies. The Eborsisk monster at the end is stop motion whilst a transformation scene utilises the computer technique of morphing to make a smooth transformation. Three years later, ILM perfected the technique in *Terminator 2: Judgement Day*. *Willow* is a very believable movie with strong performances but it is a little spoilt by some weak humour. Thematically, the film ties in with *Star Wars* with its everyday protagonist who achieves greatness through a combination of commitment to a cause and some intervention from the world of magic. In an interview with *Starlog* (issue 132), Ron Howard suggests that *Willow* explores many of the same issues as *Star Wars* but through a female perspective. In the *Willow Official Theatre Programme*, Howard states: "[George] wanted a movie about people and their emotions. From the very start of the project, he wanted a real human touch - despite the fact there aren't very many literal humans in *Willow*." The character of Fin Raziel is very much in the spirit of Obi-Wan Kenobi. For comic relief, Lucas gives the story Franjean and Rool - two nine-inch-high characters whose comic schtick is not so far removed from those of Jar-Jar Binks. General Kael/Darth Vader is subservient to Queen Bavmorda/The Emperor, who is driven by selfishness and ultimately fear. In interviews with Lucas, it is clear that he relishes the opportunity to create worlds that can only exist and live on film. In a sense his film-making is not about photographing reality but building realities from scratch which are then given human emotions and interests.

Willow did not prove the hit that had perhaps been hoped. In the mid-1990s, Lucas followed up the film with a trilogy of novels written by Chris Claremont from a story sequence by Lucas: *Shadow Dawn*, *Shadow Moon* and *Shadow Star*. The stories follow Elora Danan as a young woman aided by Willow Ufgood, now living under the name of Thorn Drumheller. The novel trilogy begins thirteen years after the events depicted in the feature film. Evidently, the *Willow* feature film was intended to have had a more powerful impact and continue as a movie series. The film's marketing campaign pushed the magic and mystery. A beautiful teaser poster comprised solely of swirling red light with the words 'Forget all you know, or think you know' maybe did not say enough. A second montage poster of faces accompanied the release very much in the format of other Lucasfilm release posters.

Lucas' other 1988 release was a smaller movie that fizzed with energy and optimism. It was no big deal at the time but is now regarded as one of the best films of the 1980s. The film was *Tucker: The Man And His Dream*, a biopic of the man who designed a car in the 1940s which threatened the Big Three American motor companies of the time. The film was directed by Francis Ford Coppola and was regarded as something of an autobiographical film by both Lucas and Coppola, being a celebration of the maverick mindset. *Tucker* is a very strong film and it is a pity it is almost forgotten because it boldly states many ideas Lucas is committed to in his film-making. Lucas has stated that he wishes he could have made other films on this scale. Maybe Lucas has been trapped by his own success.

Tucker: The Man And His Dream, starred Jeff Bridges (as Preston Tucker), Joan Allen and Lloyd Bridges. Although Coppola had been keen to develop the film since the 1970s, he approached Lucas in 1985 to see if he was interested in producing it. Lucas saw the story had allusions to his and Coppola's work as independent film-makers with Zoetrope and beyond that. Lucas' key contribution was to define a clear storyline and to focus on a main theme, the maverick making his way in the world, his fighting spirit fuelling him all the way. The film is suffused with rich images, rather like the glitzy, polished look of 1940s advertising. In an interview in *Premiere* (August 1988), Coppola referred to "George's almost scientific talent for story construction." Tucker is a classic Lucas character, a maverick in favour of the new and the progressive. In the film he even has a mentor figure, Uncle Abe Kravitz. The finished film is energetic and cinematic and a salute to creativity and thinking differently. Lushly shot by Vittorio Storaro and with a funky, peppy score by Joe Jackson, *Tucker* is a celebration of the little guy fighting the system.

In 1988, again with Coppola, Lucas executive-produced a film called *Powaqqatsi*, sequel to the seminal 1982 film *Koyaanisqatsi*. Both films were directed by Godfrey Reggio and one has to imagine that they are the kind of abstract films Lucas himself would be keen to direct and piece together someday. *Powaqqatsi* is Hopi for 'life out of balance,' interestingly enough an issue that *The Phantom Menace* articulates. One senses that Reggio's style with this film goes back to the pure film ideal that Lucas started out with. *Powaqqatsi* presents images of the natural world juxtaposed with images of the so-called developed, industrial world. As with *Koyaanisqatsi*, this film is scored by Philip Glass. Somewhat touchingly, Lucas displayed a certain bewilderment and frustration in the BBC1 documentary *Flying Solo* when he wondered why journalists never spoke to him about films like *Powaqqatsi*, *Mishima* or *Kagemusha*. Maybe Lucas wishes and hopes that film history will record that his contributions to cinema extend beyond the fast thrills and wide-eyed wonder of *Star Wars* and *Indiana Jones*.

Again demonstrating his interest in supporting and encouraging films for young people, Lucas teamed with Steven Spielberg as executive producers on one of the best classically animated films of the past twenty years, *The Land Before Time*, telling the story of young dinosaurs (Littlefoot, Cera, Spike, Petrie and Ducky) seeking refuge from the ravages of the changing world as they trek to find the lush Great Valley. The storyline is elemental and gracefully told with a terrific score by James Horner. Dialogue is near meaningless as the visuals speak for themselves. Lucas' major contribution to the project was the characterisation of the strong-willed female triceratops, Cera. The film taps into basic emotions of family and commitment to a cause and a sense of community. The film was a big hit. We can only hope that

Lucas involves himself again in bringing feature animation to the screen. This was not his only experience of helping bring dinosaurs to the screen. In early 1993, Spielberg asked Lucas to supervise post-production on *Jurassic Park* whilst Spielberg went to Poland to shoot *Schindler's List*. As a result, Lucas receives a special thanks credit at the end of *Jurassic Park*. Lucas' time spent hanging around *Jurassic Park* in post-production galvanised his feeling that computer-generated images were complex, subtle and believable enough now to move ahead with a return to the world of *Star Wars*.

One Last Ride Gets You Back Home

The mainstream press perceived Lucas' film-making efforts since 1984 to have been a little inconsistent conceptually and commercially, and saw the return to *Indiana Jones* to be an effort to reassert his mastery of the audience. Having gone through various permutations to a story for Indy including one about an African Monkey King and another with something of a haunted house element, Lucas developed a story around the Holy Grail and handed it over to the late Jeffrey Boam to write a screenplay. Steven Spielberg once again directed. The most attention in development of the project was given to creating a believable sparring yet warm relationship between Indy and his father, Henry. The approach worked and gave the adventure format a real strength, making it the most emotionally satisfying and amusing Indy movie.

Indiana Jones and the Last Crusade was the last Lucas feature film for several years as he turned his attention to television.

The first live-action TV project since *Ewoks: The Battle For Endor* was *Maniac Mansion*, based on the popular Lucasfilm Games Division computer game. Typically, Lucas served as executive producer on the programme which was essentially a comedy about a family of inventors called the Edisons.

One project which regrettably did not come to pass after much development work was *Redtails*, a historical drama about The Tuskegee airmen during the Second World War. The Tuskegee pilots were a corps of black airmen who flew countless missions. Lucas was to have executive-produced but sadly the project never lifted off.

Indiana Jones: Boy Adventurer

Through his engagement with educational computer programming Lucas developed an idea around history and soon realised that the character of Indiana Jones would be an appropriate way to funnel stories of the past. Consequently *The Young Indiana Jones Chronicles* TV series was launched in 1992. It was not driven by thrilling action or the intervention of the unknown but was instead a kind of biography of Indiana Jones as a young person. Some episodes dealt with Indy as a little boy aged about nine whilst other installments followed Indy as a young man through the period around the First World War. The series had an epic span and also proved a testing ground for much of the digital film-making technology later applied in the spruced-up *Star Wars Special Editions* and also in the *Star Wars* prequel stories.

The Young Indiana Jones Chronicles made history very accessible, particularly to young people. Each week Indy encountered a real historical figure such as TE Lawrence or Ernest Hemingway or Albert Schweitzer. The second season of the show even features Harrison Ford as a bearded Indy looking back on his adventures. Lucas' intention was for each story to be character rather than action driven, like *The Wonder Years* for example. Lucas was executive producer, conceived all the screen stories and then worked with a cadre of scriptwriters at Skywalker Ranch as well as overseeing post-production. Many of the writers went on to successful feature film screenwriting careers, notably Frank Darabont. In an interview with Bill Warren for *Starlog*, Darabont stated that one of the reasons Lucas designed the series was that Lucas "[is] truly a history buff, and is disturbed by the fact that history isn't very well taught in this country. I think, in a way, that George probably equates adventure and learning as being part and parcel of the same thing, as being part of the same experience."

The series marked the beginning of Lucas' collaboration with Rick McCallum as producer and part of the show's mission was to explore the capabilities and limitations of digital effects to reduce the costs of location and extras. Nonetheless, the project was shot around the world with its stories of Indy interacting with famous historical figures. Initially each episode was framed by Indy as a very old man reminiscing about a given exploit to a group of young people but this might have been a little patronising. The series had an ever-present romantic aspect to it. Indy often fell in love as he globe-trotted. It was this series along with the George Lucas Educational Foundation which perhaps marked him as a film-maker with a desire to serve very clearly as a teacher. Since airing in the early 1990s the series has been released on video where episodes have been joined together to create feature-length mini movies. The series, whilst being recognised for its intelligence and high production value, never really had a big audience. Perhaps people thought they were getting the cinema incarnation of Indiana Jones rather than what Lucas wanted to deliver. Interestingly, the young Indiana Jones is once more the typical Lucas hero who is young, bright eyed and endlessly enquiring and questioning, just like Curt Henderson, just like Luke Skywalker, just like the boy Anakin Skywalker. The series is one of Lucas' finest pieces of work and one which most people are unaware of. For Frank Darabont, the significance of *The Young Indiana Jones Chronicles* was not just in the subject, but that it fired up Lucas again as a film-maker so that he was able to return to the world that had shaped so many young imaginations.

The More Things Change
The More They Stay The Same

The George Lucas Super Live Adventure further cemented Lucas' pop culture standing. It was a compilation stage performance of Lucas' movies which toured Japan in 1993. The show's narrative was built around the conceit of a young woman being transported from the theatre audience and into the various worlds of Lucas' films. The stage show included a huge castle set, a vast jukebox, a Death Star set and a night-club set. There were action set pieces, swordfighting, dancing and even an appearance from Darth Vader. Orchestral music accompanied the immense production which to date has only ever been seen in Japan, where Lucas has a huge following.

In 1994, Lucas released *Radioland Murders*, a movie with a very long history. It had been developed by Lucas in the early 1970s and sat on the shelf for many years. At one point in the late 1980s Ron Howard considered directing the movie. When it finally went into production, the director was Mel Smith. Rick McCallum produced and Lucas provided the screen story and served as executive producer and overseer. The film was made for about $10 million. It features no 'name' actors and Lucas once again explored the potential of Industrial Light and Magic's application of digital technology to create an illusion of scale and believability of setting. The film implemented a new visual effects tool, the SABRE system, which rendered effects in real time. The many dancers were created by multiplying just a handful, and the digital backlot was used again after the initial experiments on *The Young Indiana Jones Chronicles*. The energy of so many of his movies once again fuels *Radioland Murders* as two radio drama writers frantically launch the opening night of a Chicago radio station whilst simultaneously unravelling a murder mystery on the premises. Lucas goes for a screwball effect and lots of fast and snappy dialogue which certainly reveals the influence of screenwriters Willard Huyck and Gloria Katz on the film. The spats between the hero and heroine recalls Han and Leia's bickering in *A New Hope*. The film is busy and almost relentlessly so, as once again Lucas seeks to tell a story as fast as he can without losing the audience. Even in this very light and fluffy movie, the familiar Lucas theme of community shines through as everybody bands together to ensure success.

Shortly after the release of *Radioland Murders*, Lucas sat down and began drafting the screenplay for *The Phantom Menace*. Whilst working on the screenplay and developing the prequel series, Lucas had also begun work revising the original series, encouraged by the technology employed on *Jurassic Park*. The *A New Hope Special Edition* was released in January 1997, *The Empire Strikes Back* in February 1997 and *Return Of The Jedi* in March 1997. Each film did very strong business for such oft-viewed films and only served to show just how popular the *Star Wars* story remained. It was also an opportunity for Lucas to test out the fundamental issues of computer-generating characters in anticipation of the *Star Wars* prequels. Jar-Jar Binks took eighteen months before a final design was approved for the character who appears in around 400 shots. Binks represents the latest iteration in the integration of live action and animation which reaches right back to the

1920s with the efforts of Walt Disney's *Alice* comedies, the Fleischer Studios' *Out Of The Inkwell* series, through to *Mary Poppins* and on to *Young Sherlock Holmes*, *Who Framed Roger Rabbit?*, *The Abyss* and *Jurassic Park*.

Star Wars received the biggest overhaul for the *Special Edition* project with its inclusion of an exchange between Han Solo and Jabba the Hutt. It had been filmed in 1976 but the technology and time had not been available to create Jabba. For the *Special Edition*, Lucas even included Boba Fett in the scene, once again showing Lucas' ambition to make *Star Wars* one very big story in which certain characters drop in and out of the narrative over a period of years - Boba Fett appears as a child in *Attack Of The Clones*. Lucas also expanded the scope of Mos Eisley and notably included a warm, pastoral establishing shot of Ben Kenobi's remote hideaway and many more stormtoopers facing Han Solo as he runs around a corner.

The Empire Strikes Back had the least revisions. For the snow battle, transparencies in the matte process were eliminated. The Hoth Wampa was shown more effectively and explicitly and the hallways of Cloud City were given windows and views of the city beyond. Thankfully, Phil Tippett and John Berg's glorious stop motion work was not deemed ripe for a digital overhaul, thereby retaining the film's correct place in the history of visual effects development. In the *Special Edition* Luke Skywalker now wails as he falls to his apparent doom at the end of the movie.

Return Of The Jedi's restoration was similarly minimal. The Sarlaac was made more ferocious and most notably Lucas included a sweeping montage of environments for the triumphant finale.

Placed in the context of the digital age, the *Special Editions* are fascinating pre-digital parades of visual effects. Seeing the films on the big screen as opposed to video also allowed audiences to somehow feel the stories breathe again - refreshed and reinvigorated.

As of this writing and in keeping with Lucas' ongoing revisions of his work, the word is that in 2006 (a year after the release of *Episode III* which Lucas is writing at present with design work just underway) Lucas will re-release the second trilogy again with additional scenes and amendments so that it ties in completely and comprehensively with the prequel stories. Quite what this will mean in terms of specific scenes and inclusions is unknown at this point.

In 1999, Lucas released *The Phantom Menace*, which dominated the pop culture landscape for virtually most of the year. Lucas began crafting the next instalment and continued to develop the Letterman Army Hospital site at The Presidio site in San Francisco. The plan is to create a digital arts complex. "We think the arts should be represented in parks," Lucas commented to *The Wall Street Journal* in an interview in early 2001.The Letterman Digital Arts Centre will house ILM, THX, LucasArts and The George Lucas Educational Foundation.

Occasionally quizzed about his plans for after the completion of the *Star Wars* cycle, Lucas says he would like to return to the format of television and perhaps something with an historical setting. He has not spoken much of a fourth Indiana Jones film although in an autumn 2001 *Empire* magazine special Steven Spielberg said he would like a fourth bullwhip adventure to explore the aging process, rather in the way that Richard Lester's *Robin And Marian* (1976) did. After *Star Wars: Episode III*, Lucas wants to explore ideas that have been percolating over the past few decades, possibly focusing on TV- and internet-based material.

Lucas' Legacy

Lucas is in the intriguing position of having been responsible for two immense pop culture contributions: first the stories he has told and second the way his foresight and collaborations with technologists have revised the way films can be made. In a way he is both software and hardware king. He is as famous for his creation of Industrial Light and Magic and the Skywalker Ranch as he is for the creations that have come out of it. He has shown how education can be augmented by movie style and computer game-driven aesthetics so that education and a sense of play (in the best sense) combine. His charity The George Lucas Educational Foundation is committed to interfacing the formal educational environment with digital technology. LucasArts Games have created a range of educational software based around *The Phantom Menace*. Skywalker Sound is a post-production facility and THX

Recording is a prestigious seal of approval and quality. In so many of his interviews, Lucas seems to prefer talking about the presentation of films rather than the ideas contained in the stories.

Lucas has frequently stated that film has now become much more of a painterly medium, rather than a photographic one. This challenges the long-held faith in cinema's inherent photographic realism. Yet, even the simplest, most austere close-up of a human face is as fake as the widest vista of a galaxy. Neither are really there as you watch them; they are just projected images.

In Lucas' story world, determination, clear thinking and commitment will see you through. If you can cope with the fast and the furious then you'll be okay. If you can trust in what you can't see then that's fine too. Like Frank Capra on a galactic scale, Lucas' best efforts have promoted the victory of the small over the big. Never take appearances for what they are, many of Lucas' films say, and that realisation might open up all sorts of vistas and connections. Who would know that mild Professor Indiana Jones is a heroic adventurer. Or that Wolfman Jack is the fount of all knowledge. Or that the world beyond The White Limbo is, as THX discovered, beautiful.

Lucas' consistency as a writer/director reveals him as a true auteur, just like Bergman, Ozu, Scorsese, Ford, Welles and so many others. Reluctance on people's part to admit this speaks less of their appreciation of Lucas' skills and more of the prejudice that perhaps still exists towards the once highly-disreputable genres of fantasy, science fiction and pulp adventure.

So what is that defining Lucas image? That ultimate moment? Is it Luke rejecting anger and violence? Is it Indiana Jones kneeling in his humility on his way to the Holy Grail? For all the spectacle and fantasy maybe the key image is the most low-key. It is of Curt Henderson, at the end of *American Graffiti*, gazing out of the airplane window and remembering all that has been and imagining all that can happen.

Reference Materials

Books:

Once Upon A Galaxy: A Journal Of The Making Of The Empire Strikes Back, Alan Arnold, Sphere Books, 1980, ISBN 0722156529

George Lucas, John Baxter, HarperCollins, 1999, ISBN 9780002570091

The Making Of Star Wars: The Phantom Menace, Laurent Bouzereau & Jody Duncan, Random House/Ebury Press, May 1999, ISBN 9780091868673

Star Wars: The Annotated Screenplays, Laurent Bouzereau, Titan Books, 1998, ISBN 9781852869236

The Art Of Star Wars: The Phantom Menace, Jonathan Bresman, Ballantine Books/Ebury Press, 1999, ISBN 009186870X

The Art Of The Empire Strikes Back, Deborah Call,Vic Bulluck & Valerie Hoffman, Ballantine, 1980, ISBN 0345332172

The Power Of Myth, Joseph Campbell with Bill Moyers, Doubleday Books, 1989, ISBN 9780385247740

George Lucas: The Creative Impulse, 2nd Edition, Charles Champlin, Virgin Books, 1997, ISBN 9781852 277215

Emotional Intelligence, Daniel Goleman, Bloomsbury, 1996, ISBN 9780747528302

Shadow Dawn, Chris Claremont & George Lucas, Bantam Books, 1998, ISBN 055357289X

Shadow Moon, Chris Claremont & George Lucas, Bantam Books, 1995 ISBN 0553504266

Shadow Star, Chris Claremont & George Lucas, Bantam Books, 2000, ISBN 0553572881

Pocket Essentials: Steven Spielberg, James Clarke, Oldcastle Books, 2001, ISBN 1903047439

The Future Of The Movies: Interviews With Martin Scorsese, Steven Spielberg And George Lucas, Roger Ebert & Gene Siskel, Andrews and McMeel Books, 1991, ISBN 0836262166

Postmodern Auteurs: Coppola, Lucas, De Palma, Spielberg And Scorsese, Kenneth von Gunden, McFarland, 1991, ISBN 0899506186

Attack Of The Clones: The Illustrated Companion, Marcus Hearn, Ebury Press, 2002, ISBN 0091884780

Star Wars: The Magic Of Myth, Mary Henderson, Ballantine, 1997, ISBN 0553507052

Zen In The Art Of Archery, Eugen Herrigel, Penguin Arkana, 1988, ISBN 0140190740

George Lucas: Interviews, Sally Kline (Ed), University of Mississippi Press, 1999, ISBN 1578061253

The Making Of Return Of The Jedi, John Philip Peecher, Ballantine Del Rey, 1983, ISBN 034531235X

Zen Flesh, Zen Bones, Paul Reps (Ed), Penguin, 2000, ISBN 014028832

George Lucas: Close Up, Chris Salewicz, OrionMedia, 1998, ISBN 9780752813189

Star Wars: From Concept To Screen To Collectable, Steven J Sansweet, Chronicle Books, 1992, ISBN 9780811800969

Star Wars Scrapbook: The Essential Collection, Steven J Sansweet, Virgin Books, 1998, ISBN 9781852277024

Regeneration Through Violence: The Mythology Of The American Frontier 1600-1860, Richard Slotkin, University of Oklahoma Press, 2000, ISBN 9780806132297

Industrial Light And Magic: The Art Of Special Effects, Thomas G Smith, Columbus Books, 1988, ISBN 0862871425

Biographical Dictionary Of Film, David Thompson, Andre Deutsch Ltd, 1995, ISBN 9780233989532

The Art Of Star Wars, Carol Titelman, Ballantine, November 1979, ISBN 0345352084

From Star Wars To Indiana Jones: The Best Of The Lucasfilm Archives, Mark Cotta Vaz & Shinji Hata, Chronicle Books, 1994, ISBN 0811809722

Industrial Light And Magic: Into The Digital Realm, Mark Cotta Vaz & Patricia Rose Duignan, Virgin Books, 1996, ISBN 1852276061

The Art Of Star Wars: Attack Of The Clones, Mark Cotta Vaz, Lucas Books/ Ebury Press, 2002, ISBN 0091884691

The Art Of Return Of The Jedi, Ballantine, 1983, ISBN 034530957X

Official Tie-In Books

Bantha Tracks, various numbers, 1978-1984, quarterly published by Lucasfilm

The Empire Strikes Back: Official Collectors' Edition, Paradise Press, 1980

Indiana Jones and the Last Crusade: Official Collectors' Edition, Dennis Oneshots Ltd, 1989

Indiana Jones and the Temple of Doom: Official Collectors' Edition, Paradise Press, 1984

Lucasfilm Fan Club Magazine, established 1987, changed title to *Star Wars Insider*, autumn 1994. Issues 1, 2, 3, 7, 15, 18, 20, 21

Official Star Wars Magazine UK, Number 1 April/May 1996 - present, Titan Publishing

Raiders Of The Lost Ark Collectors' Album, George Fenmore Associates, 1981

Return Of The Jedi: Official Collectors' Edition, Paradise Press, 1983

Star Wars: Official Collectors' Edition, Marvel, 1977

The Phantom Menace, Official Souvenir Edition, Titan Magazines, 1999

Star Wars Insider, Issues 23 to present, 1994 - 2000. Published by Wizards of the Coast 2000 onwards.

Willow: The Official Movie Magazine, Starlog Press, 1988

Willow: The Official Theatre Programme, 1988, *Starlog Press*

Articles

Susan Adamo, interview with Mark Hamill, *Starlog* 65, December 1982, pp 18-22

Benjamin Bergery, 'Digital Cinema by George,' *American Cinematographer*, September 2001

Emma Brockes, 'No, *Star Wars* Is Not Supposed To Be Funny,' *The Guardian*, 16 May 2002

Scott Chernoff and Kevin Fitzpatrick, 'Lucas Takes Manhattan,' *Star Wars: The Official Magazine*, October/November 1999, pp 20-23

Gerald Clarke, 'Star Wars 3: Return Of The Jedi: George Lucas and Friends Wrap It All Up/Great Galloping Galaxies,' *Time*, 23 May 1983, pp 30-37

Gerald Clarke, 'The Empire Strikes Back,' *Time*, 19 May 1980, pp 58-63

Gerald Clarke, 'I've Got to get My Life Back Again,' *Time*, 23 May 1983, pp 38-40

Richard Corliss, 'Ready, Set, Glow!,' *Time*, 31 May 1999, pp 52-63

Richard Corliss & Jess Cagle, 'Dark Victory,' *Time*, 29 April 2002, pp 48-59

Richard Downes, 'Jedi Knight Fever,' *Radio Times*, 3-9 July 1999, pp 24-27

Lee Jancee Dunn, 'A Star Is Born,' *Rolling Stone*, 24 June 1999, pp 41-46

Richard Dyer, 'Making Star Wars Sing Again,' *Boston Globe*, 28 March 1999

Ian Freer, 'Interview with George Lucas,' *Empire*, September 1999, pp 114-122

Lee Goldberg, 'George Lucas: The New Projects,' *Starlog* 100, November 1985, pp 42-43

Lee Goldberg, 'The Ewok Adventure,' *Starlog* 89, December 1984, pp 61-63, 67

Lee Goldberg, 'John Korty: Director Of The Ewok Adventure,' *Starlog* 90, January 1985, pp 27-29

Bruce Handy, 'The Force Is Back,' *Time*, 17 March 1997, pp 79-84

Simon Hattenstone, 'Who's Afraid of Steven Spielberg?...He Is,' *The Guardian*, 11 September 1998, p 4

Aljean Hermetz, 'Burden of Dreams,' *American Film*, June 1983, pp 30-36

David Hutchinson, 'Into the Third Dimension With Captain Eo,' *Starlog* 115, February 1987, pp 63-68, 73

David Kamp, 'The Force Is Back,' *Vanity Fair*, February 1999, pp 58-72

David Kamp, 'Love In A Distant Galaxy,' *Vanity Fair*, March 2002, p 96

Kevin Kelly and Paula Parisi, 'Beyond Star Wars,' *Wired*, February 1997, pp 72-77, 102, 104, 106

Randy and Jean-Marc Lofficier, 'The Primoridal Star Wars,' *Starlog* 120, July 1987, pp 17-20

Brian Lowry, 'Was it Hot In the Costume?,' *Starlog* 99, October 1985, pp 23-26, 72

George Lucas, 'The Future of Film,' *Premiere*, February 1999, pp 59-60

Dan Madsen, 'The Force Behind Lucasfilm,' *Lucasfilm Fan Club Magazine* 8, pp 2-6, 13

Dan Madsen, 'The Future Of The Force,' *Lucasfilm Fan Club Magazine* 17, pp 2-6

Bill Moyers, 'Of Myth and Men,' *Time*, 26 April 1999

Steve Oney, 'Coppola's Tucker,' *Premiere*, August 1988, pp 68-74

Paula Parisi, 'Grand Illusion,' *Wired*, May 1999, pp 137-139

Adam Pirani, 'Warwick Davis-Return Of The Ewok,' *Starlog* 101, December 1985, pp 29-31

Adam Pirani, 'Ron Howard: Storyteller of Shadow and Magic,' *Starlog* 132, July 1988, pp 33-39

William Rabkin, 'Howard the Duck Goes Hollywood,' *Starlog* 110, September 1986, pp 45-47

Tim Rayment, 'Master Of The Universe,' *Sunday Times*, 16 May 1999, pp 14-24

Orville Schell, 'George and His Dragons,' *The Observer*, 25 April 1999, pp 1-2

Steve Silberman, 'G Force,' *Wired*, May 1999, pp 133-35, 182

Ian Spelling, 'Life with Indy,' *Starlog* 191, June 1993, pp 46-49

Anne Thompson, 'The Big Bang,' *Premiere*, May 1999, pp 68-77

Bill Warren, 'George Lucas: Father Of The Force,' *Starlog* 127, February 1988

Bill Warren, 'Chronicling the Young Indiana Jones,' *Starlog* 178, May 1992, pp 52-55, 69

Cinefantastique, February 1997, *Star Wars*
Cinefex 65, 78
American Cinematographer, September 1999, *The Phantom Menace*
Dreamwatch 59, Summer 1999, *The Phantom Menace*
Empire 122, August 1999, *The Phantom Menace*
'Star Wars: The Year's Best Movie,' *Time*, 30 May 1977
Star Wars Insider Magazine, Autumn 1997, pp 14-17
The Sunday Times Magazine, 16 May 1999, *Star Wars*
Total Film 31, August 1999, pp 52-66, *The Phantom Menace*

TV:

Flying Solo: March 1997, *Omnibus*, BBC1
The Story Of Star Wars, 7 July 1999, *Omnibus,* BBC1
The Making Of Star Wars, 1977, VHS 5013738105256
From Star Wars To Jedi: The Making Of A Saga, 1983, VHS 5013738147959

Videos & DVDs

Lucas as Writer/Director

THX 1138 VHS S014005
American Graffiti DVD UDR 90076
A New Hope VHS 21365W (*The Star Wars Trilogy Widescreen* boxset, 2000 edition)
The Phantom Menace VHS 14246W/DVD 22733DVD

As Producer/Executive Producer

The Empire Strikes Back VHS 21365W
Return Of The Jedi VHS 21365W
The Adventures Of Indiana Jones: Raiders Of The Lost Ark, Indiana Jones And The Temple Of Doom, Indiana Jones And The Last Crusade VHR 4395
Mishima deleted
Labyrinth VHS CC8166/DVD CDR 97209
Howard The Duck deleted
Tucker: The Man And His Dream DVD Region 1 B00004Y62
Willow DVD Region 1 B00003CXD
The Land Before Time VHS 0446773

Soundtracks

American Graffiti MCLDD19150
A New Hope CD 09026687722 RCA Victor
The Empire Strikes Back CD 09026687732 RCA Victor
Return Of The Jedi CD 09026687742 RCA Victor
The Phantom Menace CD SK61816 Sony
The Phantom Menace Special Edition CD S2K89460 Sony
Attack Of The Clones, SK89965 Sony Classical
Raiders Of The Lost Ark CD Raiders 001 Silva
Indiana Jones And The Temple Of Doom Audio Cassette POLHC8 821592-4 Polydor
Indiana Jones And The Last Crusade CD 7599 25883 2 Warner Bros.
Labyrinth CDFA3322
Willow CDV2538 Virgin Movie Music
Tucker: The Man And His Dream Audio Cassette AMC3917
The Land Before Time MCD06266
Radioland Murders MCAD 11159 MCA
Powaqqatsi WEA/Atlantic/Nonesuch B0000051Z8
Mishima WEA/Atlantic/Nonesuch B0000051XM
The Young Indiana Jones Chronicles Varese Sarabande B000008GT0

Websites

www.starwars.com - The official Lucasfilm website for the *Star Wars* saga, detailing all things cinematic, literary and otherwise. A treasure trove of information, behind-the-scenes features and video, trailers, breaking news.

www.theforce.net - One of the most comprehensive *Star Wars* fansites.

www.lucasfilm.com - Lucasfilm's official homepage, including details of their proposed digital media facility in San Francisco.

www.drewstruzan.com - Official page for the ultimate *Star Wars* poster artist.

www.dougchiang.com - Official page for the *Star Wars* prequel conceptual artist.

www.ralphmcquarrie.com - Official page for the original *Star Wars* conceptual artist.

www.indianajones.com - Official Lucasfilm website for the *Indiana Jones* films.

www.theraider.net - Comprehensive page about Indiana Jones.

www.glef.org - Site for The George Lucas Educational Foundation.

The Essential Library: Best-Sellers

Build up your library with new titles every month

Alfred Hitchcock (2nd Edition) by Paul Duncan

More than 20 years after his death, Alfred Hitchcock is still a household name, most people in the Western world have seen at least one of his films, and he popularised the action movie format we see every week on the cinema screen. He was both a great artist and dynamite at the box office. This book examines the genius and enduring popularity of one of the most influential figures in the history of the cinema!

Stanley Kubrick (2nd Edition) by Paul Duncan

Kubrick's work, like all masterpieces, has a timeless quality. His vision is so complete, the detail so meticulous, that you believe you are in a three-dimensional space displayed on a two-dimensional screen. He was commercially successful because he embraced traditional genres like War (*Paths Of Glory, Full Metal Jacket*), Crime (*The Killing*), Science Fiction (*2001*), Horror (*The Shining*) and Love (*Barry Lyndon*). At the same time, he stretched the boundaries of film with controversial themes: underage sex (*Lolita*); ultra violence (*A Clockwork Orange*); and erotica (*Eyes Wide Shut*).

Orson Welles (2nd Edition) by Martin Fitzgerald

The popular myth is that after the artistic success of *Citizen Kane* it all went downhill for Orson Welles, that he was some kind of fallen genius. Yet, despite overwhelming odds, he went on to make great Films Noirs like *The Lady From Shanghai* and *Touch Of Evil*. He translated Shakespeare's work into films with heart and soul (*Othello, Chimes At Midnight, Macbeth*), and he gave voice to bitterness, regret and desperation in *The Magnificent Ambersons* and *The Trial*. Far from being down and out, Welles became one of the first cutting-edge independent film-makers.

Woody Allen (2nd Edition) by Martin Fitzgerald

Woody Allen: Neurotic. Jewish. Funny. Inept. Loser. A man with problems. Or so you would think from the characters he plays in his movies. But hold on. Allen has written and directed 30 films. He may be a funny man, but he is also one of the most serious American film-makers of his generation. This revised and updated edition includes *Sweet And Lowdown* and *Small Time Crooks*.

Film Noir by Paul Duncan

The laconic private eye, the corrupt cop, the heist that goes wrong, the femme fatale with the rich husband and the dim lover - these are the trademark characters of Film Noir. This book charts the progression of the Noir style as a vehicle for filmmakers who wanted to record the darkness at the heart of American society as it emerged from World War to the Cold War. As well as an introduction explaining the origins of Film Noir, seven films are examined in detail and an exhaustive list of over 500 Films Noirs are listed.

The Essential Library: Currently Available

Film Directors:

Woody Allen (2nd)	Tim Burton	Ang Lee
Jane Campion*	John Carpenter	Joel & Ethan Coen (2nd)
Jackie Chan	Steve Soderbergh	Clint Eastwood
David Cronenberg	Terry Gilliam*	Michael Mann
Alfred Hitchcock (2nd)	Krzysztof Kieslowski*	Roman Polanski
Stanley Kubrick (2nd)	Sergio Leone	Oliver Stone
David Lynch	Brian De Palma*	George Lucas
Sam Peckinpah*	Ridley Scott (2nd)	
Orson Welles (2nd)	Billy Wilder	
Steven Spielberg	Mike Hodges	

Film Genres:

Blaxploitation Films	Bollywood	French New Wave
Horror Films	Spaghetti Westerns	Vietnam War Movies
Vampire Films*	Heroic Bloodshed*	
Slasher Movies	Film Noir	

Film Subjects:

Laurel & Hardy	Marx Brothers	Film Music
Steve McQueen*	Marilyn Monroe	The Oscars®
Filming On A Microbudget	Bruce Lee	

TV:

Doctor Who

Literature:

Cyberpunk	Philip K Dick	The Beat Generation
Agatha Christie	Sherlock Holmes	Noir Fiction*
Terry Pratchett	Hitchhiker's Guide (2nd)	Alan Moore

Ideas:

Conspiracy Theories	Nietzsche	UFOs
Feminism	Freud & Psychoanalysis	Bisexuality

History:

Alchemy & Alchemists	The Crusades	The Black Death
Jack The Ripper	The Rise Of New Labour	Ancient Greece
American Civil War	American Indian Wars	

Miscellaneous:

The Madchester Scene	Stock Market Essentials	Beastie Boys
How To Succeed As A Sports Agent		

Available at all good bookstores or send a cheque (payable to 'Oldcastle Books') to: **Pocket Essentials (Dept GL), 18 Coleswood Rd, Harpenden, Herts, AL5 1EQ, UK**. £3.99 each (£2.99 if marked with an *) . For each book add 50p postage & packing in the UK and £1 elsewhere.

196720